A History of Birds

*To dear Dad, who loved birds and taught me so much.
I wish you had lived to see this book.*

A History of Birds

Simon Wills

WHITE
OWL

First published in Great Britain in 2017 by
Pen & Sword White Owl
an imprint of
Pen & Sword Books Ltd
47 Church Street
Barnsley
South Yorkshire
S70 2AS

ISBN 978 1 52670 155 8

Typeset in Ehrhardt by
Mac Style Ltd, Bridlington, East Yorkshire
Printed and bound in the Malta by Gutenberg Press Ltd.

Pen & Sword Books Limited incorporates the imprints of Atlas,
Archaeology, Aviation, Discovery, Family History, Fiction, History, Maritime,
Military, Military Classics, Politics, Select, Transport,
True Crime, Air World, Frontline Publishing, Leo Cooper,
Remember When, Seaforth Publishing, The Praetorian Press,
Wharncliffe Local History, Wharncliffe Transport,
Wharncliffe True Crime and White Owl.

For a complete list of Pen & Sword titles please contact
PEN & SWORD BOOKS LIMITED
47 Church Street, Barnsley, South Yorkshire, S70 2AS, England
E-mail: enquiries@pen-and-sword.co.uk
Website: www.pen-and-sword.co.uk

Contents

Introduction

Birds are a very accessible part of the natural world, and always have been. I live on the outskirts of a large coastal city, and as I write this on an inhospitably cold and rainy day I can still look out the window and see birds. There's a blackbird rooting through leaves under a bush in the garden; half a dozen gulls sail by; there are three woodpigeons huddled against the elements in the lower branches of a tree; a robin is singing somewhere close at hand despite the weather.

Our ancestors were more connected to nature than many of us today. A greater proportion of the population lived in rural areas and less land had been cleared for building, so birds were often even more visible. This is not to say that birds were not persecuted, because they were. Tudor laws labelled many birds as vermin and rewarded those who killed them; gamekeepers shot thousands of birds indiscriminately; some species were hunted for their flesh, eggs or feathers; others were killed as sport, their eggs were taken by collectors, or people wanted to keep them as pets. There were also odd beliefs about certain birds such as owls and kingfishers which encouraged people to kill them. Some species came close to extinction in the UK such as the red kite or the great crested grebe, and a few, like the great bustard, were actually exterminated.

Inevitably, and unfortunately, a history of the human relationship with birds is often a tale of avian exploitation. However, that's not the whole story. Birds have had significant symbolic meanings for all sorts of reasons. The Christian Church was an important influencer of this. When the Medieval Church labelled lapwings as deceitful, cormorants as gluttons, and jays as gossips, then this affected our ancestors' attitudes to the natural world. Quite apart from this, the wider folklore around birds is rich and varied, and often it is difficult to know how some rather strange beliefs arose. It is easy to see why the eagle was regarded as an emblem of authority and power, but how did our ancestors come to believe that it kept a special stone in its nest with healing properties? Why did people believe that crows could foretell the future? In art and literature too, birds had symbolic associations that could be complex, and might vary according to the context: the peacock's beauty led it to symbolise vanity, but its allegedly incorruptible flesh meant it could also represent immortality.

Birds of all kinds have been kept as pets and human companions, from the humble sparrow to the beautiful parrots of the world. Birds were, and are, of economic significance too – the meat and eggs of the chicken, the feathers of the goose that were so important for centuries as writing tools, and the enormous service that many birds perform by eating pests. There were whole careers that depended on birds for falconers, fletchers and farmers.

Birds fascinated our ancestors as much as they captivate us today. For millennia they have brightened our lives with their colours, their songs, their engaging behaviour, and their flight, which has come to symbolise freedom and inspired the portrayal of angels. Our forebears wrote poetry about birds, created music because of them, worshipped and depicted them, and even bestowed magical properties upon them. It is perhaps no coincidence that some of the oldest words in the English language are the names of birds.

The world would be a miserable place without birds, and in this book I hope to show how the relationship between us and our avian counterparts has evolved. Our modern attitudes are very much shaped by our ancestors' beliefs and experiences.

Acknowledgements

So many websites now make original historical texts and images available freely to researchers and I would like to take this opportunity to thank them, and especially the following:

British Library illuminated manuscripts: www.bl.uk/catalogues/illuminatedmanuscripts,
Internet Archive: https://archive.org/
Early English Books Online: http://quod.lib.umich.edu/e/eebogroup/
Google Books: https://books.google.co.uk/
Perseus Digital Library: http://www.perseus.tufts.edu/hopper/
Wellcome Images: https://wellcomeimages.org/
University of Aberdeen for the Aberdeen Bestiary online: https://www.abdn.ac.uk/bestiary/

I'd also like to thank Scotford Lawrence, curator of the National Cycle Museum.

I am grateful to Michael Palmer of Photo Experience Days: www.photoexperience days.com who taught me how to use a new camera much better than any manual could have done.

Linne Matthews has been my editor at White Owl and I have really appreciated her patience, attention to detail, and kindness.

Finally, I would as always particularly like to thank my partner, B, who is so kind and supportive whenever I am writing a book. Every writer needs looking after!

*T*he name blackbird has been in use since at least medieval times, but our Anglo-Saxon forebears preferred the term *ouzel* (pronounced 'oozle'). For many centuries these two words were used side by side in books of natural history – 'the blackbird or ouzel' – but by the late nineteenth century it was blackbird that emerged as the dominant name.

In Scotland the bird was often known as the blackie and in certain areas of England the merle or colley, the latter probably because of its coal colour. Interestingly, eighteenth-century versions of the seasonal song *The Twelve Days of Christmas* describe blackbirds being sent on the fourth day:

> *The fourth day of Christmas*
> *My true love sent to me:*
> *Four colley birds,*
> *Three French hens,*
> *Two turtle doves*
> *And a partridge in a pear tree.*

Later adaptations seem to have changed 'colley birds' to the more widely understood 'calling birds'. Another set of famous verses to feature the blackbird is the nursery rhyme *Sing a Song for Sixpence*, which was known in the eighteenth century but may have earlier origins:

Cover and illustration from Randolph Caldecott's *Sing a Song for Sixpence*, published about 1880.

Sing a song for sixpence,
A pocket full of rye.
Four and twenty blackbirds,
Baked in a pie.
When the pie was opened
The birds began to sing;
Wasn't that a dainty dish
To set before the king.

The blackbird has inspired writers of more earnest works than nursery rhymes. Poets down the ages from Shakespeare and Spenser, to John Clare and Thomas Hardy have tried to capture something of the blackbird's song and character. Tennyson wrote an entire poem called *The Blackbird*, which opens with these lines:

O blackbird! sing me something well:
While all the neighbours shoot thee round,
I keep smooth plats of fruitful ground,
Where thou may'st warble, eat and dwell.

The bird has also inspired musicians, with multiple tracks entitled *Blackbird* being released over the years from the likes of Paul McCartney, Nina Simone, Myles Kennedy and even The Wurzels to name a few. In terms of durability, one of the most well known of these songs is *Bye Bye Blackbird*. Originally written in the 1920s by American lyricist Mort Dixon, it has been covered by numerous artists and has become a classic. Some songs featuring the blackbird use the word symbolically to represent black people's struggle for equality.

The British love of the blackbird led to it being kept as an inexpensive pet for many centuries, and it is mentioned as a caged bird in some medieval bestiaries. The strong and clear song of the male bird made it especially popular, yet some individuals were taught new tunes or even learned to speak a few words. In the early nineteenth century, books about caged birds still included the blackbird as a noted favourite with instruction that, being territorial, they required a large cage to themselves. The following instance of an especially long-lived pet blackbird was reported to the *Belfast Commercial Chronicle* in 1839:

Early nineteenth-century blackbird cage.

There is at present in the possession of Mr John Spence, of Tullaghgarley, near Ballymena, a blackbird that has arrived at the wonderful age of twenty years and nearly eight months. It was taken by him from the nest when young, and ever since has enjoyed the very best of health. It still continues to sing, and that well. He is however, beginning to show symptoms of old age – his head is getting grey, and a number of white feathers are springing up on his neck and breast.

Good enough to eat?

Blackbirds were quite commonly eaten, although not baked alive in pies despite what the nursery rhyme suggests. Inexplicably, the eating of blackbirds was promoted as a treatment for dysentery or diarrhoea. On continental Europe, diners were keen to eat the birds after the grape harvest or if they had fed on myrtle or olives as these seemed to impart improved flavour to the meat.

There is little folklore, legend or symbolism attached to the blackbird in the UK. Yet the Christian Church was keen to exploit nature for symbolic purposes and two saints in particular have been associated with this bird. The first is St Benedict, who was tempted by the Devil in the form of a blackbird. The blackbird came 'fluttering round about him and coming so near his face that he might have catched it in his hand'. This strange experience greatly disconcerted Benedict to the extent that his usually rigid focus on the work of God wavered, and he found himself sorely tempted by sexual desire. Yet the holy man did not succumb:

He stripped himself of his clothes, and casting himself upon a thicket of briars and thorns, there rolled his naked body so long that it was most pitifully rent, mangled and torn, and ran gore blood; and by this excessive and stinging pain he quenched the scorching fire which Satan had kindled in his members.

God was apparently so pleased with the saint's resistance, that Benedict was never again tempted by sex for the rest of his life.

The second saint associated with the blackbird is from Ireland. Saint Kevin was a man who lived close to nature and one day while reaching his hands up to heaven in deep supplication, a blackbird is supposed to have landed on his

Early thirteenth-century depiction of Saint Kevin and his blackbird. (*Courtesy of the British Library illuminated manuscripts collection www.bl.uk*)

outstretched palm and laid an egg there. Perhaps viewing this as a test of his devotion or at least unwilling to disturb the bird, Saint Kevin stayed in this position for days until the egg hatched. Hence many representations of this saint show him with a bird in his hand.

International perspectives

The blackbird is not only popular in the UK. In Sweden it is the country's national bird, having been voted that status in 1962 and re-affirmed by a second national poll in 2015. The nation of Kosovo in the Balkans means 'of blackbirds' and is an abbreviation for the area's original name in Serbian *kosovo polje* (field of blackbirds).

In Italy, the Days of the Merla (or days of the hen blackbird) are said to be the coldest days of the year. The precise dates vary a little according to locality but are typically the last three days of January. According to legend, blackbirds were originally white, and during these three cold days they hid in chimneys to keep warm and so became permanently blackened by the soot and smoke.

Like some other well-loved European garden birds, the blackbird was exported to far-flung fresh territories during the nineteenth century. People emigrating to Australia and New Zealand, for example, wanted to feel at home in their new surroundings and the song of the blackbird was reassuringly familiar. Now the blackbird is a well-established bird in both countries.

Blue Tit

*T*he term 'blue tit' was originally an abbreviation of blue titmouse, and the story of how we have come to use the shortened form 'tit' is quite interesting. The Anglo-Saxons called small birds of this kind by the word *mase*, which probably just meant 'little'. In time this became *mose*, and in the early middle ages, the prefix 'tit-' was added, meaning small. So the new name *titmose* actually meant small little bird. At some later point, being unaware of the word's history, it was assumed that this group of birds had been named after the mouse because of their size, fluffy appearance and quick movements, and consequently *titmose* became titmouse. In the twentieth century it was universally shortened to 'tit'.

The story of this bird's name does not end there. One of the most remarkable facts about the blue tit is the large number of different regional names it has acquired over the centuries. Perhaps this is a tribute to the bird's beauty and its endearing nature. In Scotland it has been known as the blue bonnet or blue yaup – blue bonnets were traditionally a common form of Scottish headdress, whilst 'yaup' was an old word for nimble or eager, which certainly describes the bird's very busy movements when

Pictures of birds in popular publications before the nineteenth century were not always very accurate; this image of a blue tit dates from 1756.

searching for food. Another Scottish name is blue ox-eye, maybe because the bird's dark eye stands out against its pale head. In England, blue cap has been a more common name, and since at least the sixteenth century it has also been known as the 'nun' because it seems to wear a white headband like a nun.

The blue tit is quite a vocal creature and some regional names such as the Dorset 'chintree' or Lancashire 'jitty-fa' are imitative of the bird's call; the more widespread pinnock may be another example, with 'pinn' perhaps representing the bird's sound and the suffix -ock meaning 'little'. There is a long tradition in the UK of giving human sobriquets to popular birds such as Jenny Wren, Jack Daw and so on. The blue tit has been frequently known as Tom Tit, but also Billy Biter because when captured the bird fights tenaciously and will give a fearsome nip. Other names like pinchem and Billy Nipper attest to this injurious behaviour. Hickmall is a regional name that was widely used in the West Country, and there are many others including tiddley, nope, and bluey. Chaucer mentions a bird called the 'tidife', which is also believed to refer to the blue tit.

Those who are old enough to remember milk being delivered to the doorstep in bottles will undoubtedly recall how unattended bottles would sometimes be raided by blue tits. The birds learned that pecking through the aluminium cap allowed access to the cream at the top, and in our household they were particularly drawn to the richer 'gold cap' full cream milk. Blue tits have been known for centuries as birds that will scavenge dairy products and other foods from households, and so in parts of East Anglia it was known as the pickcheese. Eighteenth-century naturalist Gilbert White commented on the bird's scavenging habits around human dwellings:

> The blue titmouse, or nun, is a great frequenter of houses, and a general devourer. Beside insects, it is very fond of flesh; for it frequently picks bones on dung-hills: it is a vast admirer of suet, and haunts butchers' shops. When a boy, I have known twenty in a morning caught with snap mousetraps, baited with tallow or suet. It will also pick holes in apples left on the ground, and be well entertained with the seeds on the head of a sunflower.

People admire the blue tit for its colourful appearance but also its agility – hanging upside down, balancing on twigs that seem far too thin to support its weight, and flitting constantly from branch to branch. The Victorian 'countryside' poet John Clare mentions the bird on several occasions in his poems. These evocative lines in *The Firetail's Nest* capture the blue tit's feeding behaviour well:

> *And then the bluecap tootles in its glee,*
> *Picking the flies from orchard apple tree*

Despite its tiny size, the blue tit also has a much-admired reputation as a pugnacious bird that will defend its corner. George Montagu published a pioneering book about British birds in 1802, and he describes the blue tit's attitude in defence of its home:

The female is tenacious of her nest and will often suffer herself to be taken rather than quit it, and will frequently return again after being taken out. Upon such an occasion it menaces the invader in a singular manner, hissing like a snake, erecting all its feathers, and uttering a noise like the spitting of a cat; and if handled, bites severely.

The blue tit is renowned for sometimes nesting in the most peculiar places, and eighteenth- and nineteenth-century naturalists competed to report the most unusual nest locations: down the shaft of a well where the birds regularly got wet; in the handle of a working water pump; inside a bottle left in the garden to dry; underground in a mouse hole; in a labourer's boot; within 2 feet of the rails at a busy mainline railway station. But surely the most bizarre nest location was described by a magazine correspondent in 1832:

Tomtit or blue titmouse. I am aware that this little bird will choose curious places for bringing up its young, but the following surpasses all I ever before heard of. Some years ago, a man of the name of Tom Otter murdered his sweetheart at a place called Drinsey Nook, in Lincolnshire. The assassin suffered the extreme penalty of the law, and [in 1805] was gibbeted near the place where he committed the fatal deed. It appears that whilst the carnivorous tomtit was feeding on the flesh of the malefactor, he had an eye to a comfortable habitation in the vicinity of so much good cheer; and as there was no hole in the gibbet post to suit his purpose, he actually took possession of the dead man's mouth, and he and his mate brought forth a brood of young cannibals; and more than that, they built there the next year and were equally successful in rearing their young. I think I hear some of your readers say, 'Come, come, Mr Woodcock; you are now dealing in the marvellous and are rather stretching it,' but I can assure you, Sir, it is correct, as I have had it corroborated by several eye-witnesses.

Notwithstanding this rather gruesome tale, the blue tit is a much-loved bird. With its spirited attitude, pretty plumage, and acrobatic behaviour it is no surprise that many people enjoy watching it and are keen to invite it into their gardens.

Chicken

*T*he chicken is the commonest bird in the world because it is bred in enormous numbers to be eaten by humans. The female is called the hen and the male is the cockerel in the UK, but the rooster in countries such as the US. The domesticated chicken is descended principally from the wild junglefowl of Asia. Although they have existed in Egypt since at least the fifteenth century BC, the chicken probably came to Europe via Asia Minor (modern Turkey) and then to Greece by around the seventh century BC. Chickens in the UK are first mentioned in writing by Julius Caesar when he describes his invasion of Britannia for the second time in 54 BC. Curiously, he says: 'They do not regard it lawful to eat the hare, and the cock, and the goose; they, however, breed them for amusement and pleasure.' As far as chickens are concerned, this may mean that they were kept principally for their eggs and for fighting.

The red junglefowl (left), the principal wild ancestor of the domestic chicken, still had much in common with the birds kept by our Tudor ancestors (right).

In most cultures, chickens were domesticated mainly to eat and for their eggs, but in certain ancient civilisations they could have important religious functions too. Chickens were one of a number of animals that might be sacrificed to appease the gods, but the Greeks, Etruscans and Romans, for example, believed that chickens could also foretell the will of the Gods. Determining whether a particular action would have divine endorsement was called taking the auspices, and in military operations the Romans relied almost exclusively on chickens. These birds were taken around on campaigns under the care of a person called a *pullarius*. He would open their cage before going into battle and throw food to the chickens. If they refused to come out, did not eat, uttered a cry, or beat their wings then the signs were unfavourable and it was recommended not to join battle. However, if the chickens ate greedily it was considered a sign of divine favour, especially if some of the food fell from the birds' mouths and struck the ground.

Roman leaders who ignored the sacred chickens did so at their peril. The consul Publius Claudius Pulcher was determined to engage the Carthaginians in a sea battle in 249 BC; however, the sacred chickens refused to eat. Enraged, Claudius snatched up the cage with the birds in and threw it over the side of his ship, saying, 'Let them drink if they don't wish to eat!' He lost the battle along with ninety-three ships, 8,000 men, and 20,000 Romans taken as prisoners. When Gaius Mancinus was appointed as consul in 137 BC, the sacred chickens issued the most dire portent possible against the appointment: they flew away and were never seen again. Mancinus lost heavily in battle later that year and was arraigned for cowardice.

Another religious connection involving the chicken is featured in the Christian Bible. At the Last Supper, Jesus listened while his disciple Peter insisted that no matter what happened he would always stand by him. But Jesus prophesied to a sceptical Peter that he would deny him three times before the next morning. After Jesus was arrested, Peter trailed him at a distance and on two occasions people accused him of being a follower of Jesus, but he denied it. Then he was confronted a third time:

> About an hour later another man insisted, saying, 'This fellow was certainly with him. Why, he is a Galilean.' 'My friend,' said Peter 'I do not know what you are talking about.' At that instant, while he was still speaking, the cock crowed, and the Lord turned and looked straight at Peter, and Peter remembered what the Lord had said to him, 'Before the cock crows today, you will have disowned me three times.' And he went outside and wept bitterly.

This story is told in each of the first four Gospels of the New Testament, and is the main reason why a cockerel is traditionally used as the weather vane on top of church spires. The cockerel reminds Christians about St Peter and encourages them to stand up for what they believe and not to deny their God.

The cockerel or chicken is also the only bird to be represented among the twelve animals that make up the Chinese zodiac. People born under this sign are said to be assertive, communicative, intelligent and busy, but inclined to be critical, bossy and eccentric.

Quite apart from religious or prophetic powers, chickens have been the basis of a surprisingly large number of medical treatments over the centuries. In medieval

A cockerel weather vane on a church spire.

times, a chicken's belly was plucked and the naked part held over a swelling or sore, such as the buboes caused by the Black Death, to transfer the poison of disease into the live bird and save the afflicted person. In other situations, if wounds were not healing satisfactorily then seventeenth-century physician Alexander Read advised:

> It is not amiss to pull the feathers from the bums of hens or cocks, and to apply them often to the wounded part; or to apply young pigeons or chickens hot, being cut asunder.

Dr Read also gave advice on treating dog bites, and stressed how important it was to determine if the dog was mad before initiating treatment. If the dog was not available to examine, then its madness could be determined from the patient's wound using chickens:

> We are to beat some walnuts and to apply them to the wound, and to suffer them to lie to it for a night's space. When they are taken away, they are to be given to a cock or a hen. If the dog hath not been mad, they shall live; but if he was mad, they shall die the day after.

There were a whole variety of other alleged medical uses for chicken meat, eggs and even its dung to treat conditions including fever, incontinence and headaches. However, since Roman times a soup or broth made from chicken was valued as a general restorative for those who were ill because it is 'easily digested and breeds good blood'. It was especially recommended for alleviating the loss of vitality caused by dysentery, and in the nineteenth century, cholera.

Given that chicken broth was so esteemed, it was only a matter of time before someone thought to combine chicken and alcohol. Sure enough, 'cock ale' became a popular drink in the seventeenth and eighteenth centuries, and was said to have medicinal qualities. A recipe from 1669 describes how the beverage was made:

> Take eight gallons of ale; take a cock and boil him well; then take four pounds of raisins-of-the-sun well stoned, two or three nutmegs, three or four flakes of mace, half a pound of dates; beat these all in a mortar, and put to them two quarts of the best sack [Spanish white wine]; and when the ale hath done working, put these in, and stop it close six or seven days, and then bottle it, and a month after, you may drink it.

Cock ale was said to be a 'provocative' – something that stimulated the appetite in debilitated persons, encouraged the expectoration of phlegm from the chest, and excited lust. It was reported as a favourite drink of William III, who preferred it to wine.

However, of all the miraculous attributes of the chicken, the most incredible was surely the tale of the evil basilisk or cockatrice. This powerful but rare lizard-like creature was believed to come from the egg of an elderly cockerel, and some sources suggest it had to be hatched by a toad. The basilisk was not large but was king of the serpents, and much feared in medieval and Tudor times: there are tales of its sudden terrifying arrival from all over Europe. Its foul stench or even its gaze caused people and animals to drop dead. The most effective actions against the beast were either to send in a weasel – the only animal that could kill it – or to get the basilisk to look at its own reflection in a mirror, which also resulted in the creature's death. One of the first to describe this deadly beast was the Roman naturalist Pliny:

perducis.

This late twelfth-century medical book shows a doctor treating a patient who has been bitten by a rabid dog; it explains that if a hen is introduced to the patient and it eats well then that predicts a healthy recovery. (*Courtesy of the British Library illuminated manuscripts collection www. bl.uk*)

It has a white spot on the head, strongly resembling a sort of a diadem. When it hisses, all the other serpents fly from it: and it does not advance its body, like the others, by a succession of folds, but moves along upright and erect upon the middle. It destroys all shrubs, not only by its contact, but those even that it has breathed upon; it burns up all the grass too, and breaks the stones, so tremendous is its noxious influence. It was formerly a general belief that if a man on horseback killed one of these animals with a spear, the poison would run up the weapon and kill, not only the rider, but the horse as well. To this dreadful monster the effluvium of the weasel is fatal, a thing that has been tried with success, for kings have often desired to see its body when killed; so true is it that it has pleased Nature that there should be nothing without its antidote. The animal is thrown into the hole of the basilisk, which is easily known from the soil around it being infected. The weasel destroys the basilisk by its odour, but dies itself in this struggle of nature against its own self.

The origins of this bizarre belief are obscure, but may have a basis in stories of snakes such as the king cobra from faraway India, which, of course, hatches from eggs and is fought and often killed by the weasel-like mongoose.

Early thirteenth-century image of the fearful basilisk that has just killed a man with its stare, and now turns its attention to a ferret. (*Courtesy of the British Library illuminated manuscripts collection www.bl.uk*)

Cockerels themselves can be very aggressive, especially towards one another, and humans have taken advantage of this fact for thousands of years. Cockfighting is a blood sport that has been staged as an entertainment since at least the time of the ancient Greeks and probably much earlier. Cockerels are renowned for being territorial, and two of them, specially bred for their strength and aggression, were thrown into a small arena called a cockpit and made to fight it out in front of the crowds. It was a popular sport for gamblers in the UK for many centuries across all social classes, and was even favoured by some monarchs: Henry VIII had his own cockpit built at Whitehall Palace and James I was so fanatical about it that he appointed his own cockmaster to arrange the sport for him and decide upon wagers. Many pubs and theatres staged regular events. Cockfighting was banned by Cromwell, reinstated during the Restoration, and then finally abolished by law in England and Wales in 1835 due to its cruelty. Birds generally fought using their beaks and the sharp spurs on their legs. Sometimes the cockerels' natural defences were augmented by sharp metal spurs fixed to their legs. They generally fought until one bird killed the other. Samuel Pepys attended a cockfight in 1663, and described it in some detail:

> I to my Lord's, but he not being within, took coach, and, being directed by sight of bills upon the walls, I did go to Shoe Lane to see a cock-fighting at a new pit there, a sport I was never at in my life; but, Lord! to see the strange variety of people,

from Parliament-man (by name Wildes, that was Deputy Governor of the Tower when Robinson was Lord Mayor) to the poorest 'prentices, bakers, brewers, butchers, draymen, and what not; and all these fellows one with another in swearing, cursing, and betting. I soon had enough of it, and yet I would not but have seen it once, it being strange to observe the nature of these poor creatures, how they will fight till they drop down dead upon the table, and strike after they are ready to give up the ghost, not offering to run away when they are weary or wounded past doing further …

Sometimes a cock that has had ten to one against him will by chance give an unlucky blow, will strike the other starke dead in a moment, that he never stirs more; but the common rule is, that though a cock neither runs nor dies, yet if any man will bet £10 to a crowne, and nobody take the bet, the game is given over, and not sooner. One thing more it is strange to see how people of this poor rank, that look as if they had not bread to put in their mouths, shall bet three or four pounds at one bet, and lose it, and yet bet as much the next battle (so they call every match of two cocks), so that one of them will lose £10 or £20 at a meeting.

In the modern world, the variety of chickens available is extensive – differing greatly in appearance and behaviour from the forms that our distant ancestors would have known. People who keep chickens privately or for commercial reasons may select a particular

A cockfight in London at the beginning of the nineteenth century.

breed because of its egg-laying productivity, its size, temperament, its ability to reach maturity quickly and to put on weight, suitability to the local climate, or simply because of an attractive appearance.

The Kellogg's cockerel

Kellogg's Corn Flakes have existed since the company was founded in 1906, but the product has only featured the famous cockerel on the box from the late 1950s onwards. He is called Cornelius, or 'Corny', and is one of the most recognisable depictions of a bird in the world. There is a story, perhaps apocryphal, that a Welsh woman helped to inspire this choice of bird. Nansi Richards was a renowned international harpist who met company founder Will Kellogg, and in conversation she pointed out that his name, Kellogg, was very similar to the Welsh word for cockerel, *ceiliog*.

Four modern varieties of chicken.

Cormorant

*T*his bird's name is believed to be derived from the Latin *corvus marinus* or 'sea raven'. It has had many regional names in British seafaring communities such as the coal goose, gorma, norie, and skart. The cormorant is probably the bird most often referred to as the 'sea crow', but this title has been used in the past to denote a whole variety of other quite diverse species including the chough, razorbill, jackdaw, and even the black-headed gull. A widespread archaic variant on the cormorant's name was *corovant*.

The cormorant feeds frequently and often attempts to eat fish that appear too big to swallow. This has led to the bird becoming a metaphor for greediness. Geoffrey Chaucer, for example, wrote of the 'hot cormorant of gluttony' in the fourteenth century, whilst over 500 years later, a character in Bram Stoker's *Dracula* declares: 'I have an appetite like a cormorant.' In particular, the bird was compared with rapacious businessmen and empire-building professionals such

Mid-nineteenth-century hand-coloured print showing the 'greedy' cormorant.

as money lenders, lawyers, and even clergymen. Corn dealers came in for special abuse as they wrung indecent profits out of people who needed grain to survive; they were sometimes described by a pun on the cormorant's name: *corn vorant* ('corn devouring').

- 'The lender of money is a greedy cormorant who would swallow up the borrower.' (Daniel Sykes MP, 1824)
- 'Law is a bottomless pit; it is a cormorant, a harpy, that devours every thing.' (John Arbuthnot, 1712)
- 'Many rich cormorants (or corn-varants rather) are either childless and have no children or else they abound not in many; and yet we can see no end of their scraping, pinching, and oppressing.' (John Swan, 1635)
- 'The Irish church was a cormorant. He trusted that not one shilling more would be granted to it.' (Joseph Hume MP, 1822)

Ancient transformations

According to mythology, King Priam of Troy had a son called Aesacus who fell desperately in love. When his lover died suddenly, he threw himself off the rocks into the sea in despair, but one of the Titans took pity on him and transformed him mid-fall into a cormorant.

However, the cormorant was not only associated with greed. It is a large black bird that frequents lonely seashores, and when it stands with its wings out to dry it looks like a dark angel or even a dragon. So it is not surprising that in folklore it has acquired a slightly ominous reputation. In particular, the cormorant seems to be linked to a sense of foreboding. In his poem *Paradise Lost*, John Milton compares Satan to the bird when he arrives in the Garden of Eden. The poet describes the Devil flying up a tree where he 'sat like a cormorant'; and in this position he began 'devising death to them who lived'.

In his *Vision of the Sea*, poet Percy Shelley evokes the brute nature of an advancing storm by comparing it to various animals and he includes these lines:

> *Black as a cormorant the screaming blast,*
> *Between Ocean and Heaven, like an ocean, passed*

In *Jane Eyre*, Charlotte Brontë chooses the image of a cormorant as part of a prophetic vision. Jane paints three works of art and shows them to Mr Rochester, one of them being of a shipwreck:

> One gleam of light lifted into relief a half-submerged mast, on which sat a cormorant, dark and large, with wings flecked with foam; its beak held a gold bracelet set with gems, that I had touched with as brilliant tints as my palette could yield, and as glittering distinctness as my pencil could impart. Sinking below the bird and mast, a drowned corpse glanced through the green water; a fair arm was the only limb clearly visible, whence the bracelet had been washed or torn.

The black bird is used by Brontë to foreshadow the dark events yet to come in her story.

Sinister events in the real world have also been associated with the cormorant. On Boxing Day 1900, a replacement keeper for the remote Flannan Isle Lighthouse in the Outer Hebrides came ashore in his boat from the mainland and was surprised to find no one there to greet him. The island was reputed to be haunted, and he was overtaken by a sense of foreboding as he scrambled up the path to the lighthouse. The door was unlocked, a chair was turned over, the clocks had stopped, and the three lighthouse keepers were nowhere to be seen. They had disappeared: their fate forever a mystery. It is said that three large black birds flew away from the island – perhaps cormorants containing the souls of the three lost men. Wilfrid Wilson Gibson's poem *Flannan Isle* describes them:

> *We saw three queer, black, ugly birds –*
> *Too big, by far, in my belief,*
> *For guillemot or shag –*
> *Like seamen sitting bold upright*
> *Upon a half-tide reef:*
> *But, as we near'd, they plunged from sight,*
> *Without a sound, or spurt of white.*

There seems to have been a belief in some quarters that a cormorant landing on a church spire was especially unlucky. A cormorant was seen perched on the top of St Martin's Church in Ludgate Hill, London, in 1793, and a large crowd of concerned parishioners assembled to see it shot. A more dramatic example came at St Botolph's Church, Boston, Lincolnshire in 1860, when a big black cormorant settled on the spire. It looked sinister and people became concerned that it was a bad omen, so the church

Local people fishing with trained cormorants in the Grand Canal, Soo-Chow, China in about 1901. (*Courtesy of Library of Congress, Washington*)

custodian, Mr Hackford, shot it. As if to justify the bird's ominous reputation and the townspeople's reaction to it, a few days later the newspapers announced the unexpected death of the local MP, Herbert Ingram, and his son in a shipwreck in the US.

Yet the entirely capriciousness nature of folklore is illustrated by the fact that 250 years before the bizarre incident in Lincolnshire, a similar occurrence in Norfolk was noted without alarm. In 1608, state papers record King James I being welcomed to Thetford by three cormorants sitting on a church steeple.

These cormorants may have been some of the tame birds that the king and his successors kept for fishing. The use of cormorants to catch fish dates back many centuries and was practised particularly in China and Japan, where each fisherman might keep a dozen birds or more. The birds were released to catch fish and were either trained not to swallow them or prevented from doing so by a collar around their necks.

In 1611, John Wood was Keeper of His Majesty's Cormorants for James I and was paid £30 'for bringing up and training of certain fowls called cormorants, and making of them fit for the use of fishing'. In 1618, the cormorants were even given their own fish ponds and a brick house in which to live in the palace gardens at Westminster along with the king's otters and ospreys. The cormorants were much prized and James I gave trained birds as diplomatic gifts to various allies including King Louis XIII of France. Their value was such that the Crown compensated the Keeper of Cormorants with an award of £98 when three of them were stolen from him on the Continent by the Duke of Savoy in 1624.

Later in the seventeenth century, the ornithologist Francis Willughby described the practice of cormorant fishing in England. The birds began their day with a hood over their eyes to stop them becoming frightened or distracted while in transit to the fishing grounds:

> When they are come to the rivers they take off their hoods, and having tied a leather thong round the lower part of their necks that they may not swallow

The Liver Birds

The coat of arms of the city of Liverpool bears two birds, representing the 'liver birds' that traditionally have bestowed good fortune upon the city. The original heraldic birds awarded to the city in medieval times were probably meant to be eagles, and may have represented King John. But the medieval artwork of the earliest examples is primitive and over time, the birds' origins and identities were forgotten. By the seventeenth century, they were being recognised as cormorants, a bird commonly seen on the Mersey, and modern versions of the coat of arms clearly show them as such.

down the fish they catch, they throw them into the river. They presently dive under water, and there for a long time with wonderful swiftness pursue the fish, and when they have caught them they arise presently to the top of the water, and pressing the fish lightly with their bills they swallow them; till each bird hath after this manner devoured five or six fishes. Then their keepers call them to the fist, to which they readily fly, and little by little one after another vomit up all their fish a little bruised with the nip they gave them with their bills. When they have done fishing, setting the birds on some high place they loose the string from their necks, leaving the passage to the stomach free and open, and for their reward they throw them part of their prey they have caught, to each perchance one or two fishes, which they by the way as they are falling in the air will catch most dextrously in their mouths.

By the year 1700, British monarchs had lost interest in trained cormorants and kept them no longer. The rest of the country seems to have followed suit.

However, the art of fishing with cormorants was revived by Captain Francis Salvin in the late 1840s. He initially trained one bird, but when it died he trained more. In 1864, for example, he was using three birds named Izaak Walton, Hobble-Gobble and Detective, which he regularly took to riverside social gatherings to entertain guests. His last bird, Sub-Inspector, born in 1882, was the first known instance of a cormorant bred in confinement and was exhibited at the National Fisheries Exhibition in 1883. After Salvin's death in 1904, Sub-Inspector was sent to London Zoo and survived there until 1911. The French artist Toulouse-Lautrec fished with a cormorant named Tom who used to accompany him to bars, where the bird was encouraged to join his master in a tipple.

Crow

*T*he reputation of the crow, perhaps more than any other bird, left our ancestors in two minds. It was almost as if the bird had a split personality. On the one hand it was an intelligent creature, easily tamed, and renowned as a faithful partner and parent. However, the crow was also a bird of ill omen that was linked to death and witchcraft; it was believed to attack young farm animals such as goslings and lambs, it ate crops, and it had the disturbing habit of pecking the eyes out of corpses.

Crows have long been known for their intelligence. The Roman naturalist Pliny observed:

Nuts being too hard for their beak to break, the crow flies to a great height, and then lets them fall again and again upon the stones or tiles beneath, until at last the shell is cracked, after which the bird is able to open them.

I live not far from the sea and watch crows patrol the shore looking for winkles and cockles. They pick the molluscs up and drop them on the nearby road. If they crack open they eat them, but if not they wait for a car to do the job and then scrape up the remains. In Australia, I watched a crow waiting patiently outside a food hall. He'd learned that as soon as someone triggered the automatic doors, he could hop in after them and then patrol the tables and stalls looking for scraps. Another species of crow in North America is a well-established user of sticks as tools to catch food. Pliny gives a further example of the crow's cleverness:

A crow that was thirsty was seen heaping stones into the urn on a monument, in which there was some rainwater which it could not reach: and so, being afraid to go down to the water, by thus accumulating the stones, it caused as much water to come within its reach as was necessary to satisfy its thirst.

Crows were known to mate for life and this dedication to a single partner was admired by the Church, as was their renowned care for their offspring. The *Aberdeen Bestiary* was compiled in about 1200, and as is often the case in works of this type prepared by monks, it takes the opportunity to use an animal's behaviour as a means to give moral instruction:

Depiction of a crow from an early thirteenth-century English bestiary. (*Courtesy of the British Library illuminated manuscripts collection www.bl.uk*)

Men should learn to love their children from the practice and devotion of crows. They diligently accompany their children when flying together, anxiously supply food so that they stay strong, and do not abandon responsibility for nourishing them for a long time.

Bartholomew the Englishman, a thirteenth-century monk, recorded another example of this purported familial tenderness amongst crows:

The mildness of the bird is wonderful. For when father and mother in age are both naked and bare of covering of feathers, then the young crows hide and cover them with their feathers, and gather meat and feed them.

The crow was believed to be a divine agent. When Alexander the Great and his army became lost in a North African desert, for example, heavenly help was sent: two crows flew in front of the army and guided them to safety. In the *Quran*, Allah sent a crow to show Cain how to bury the body of his brother, Abel, whom he had just murdered, and this made him feel shame and remorse. Three-legged crows appear in both Chinese and Japanese mythology, where they have heavenly powers. Catholic tradition has it that St Paul the Hermit was brought bread every day by a crow. However, Bartholomew the Englishman warns that humans should be careful about being led by crows:

The crow is a bird of long life, and diviners [prophets] tell that she taketh heed of spyings and awaitings; and teacheth and showeth ways; and warneth what shall fall [come to pass]. But it is full unlawful to believe that God showeth His privy counsel to crows.

In *The Canterbury Tales*, Chaucer has his manciple ('provisioner') tell the story of the powerful Phoebus, who in ancient times had a much-loved wife and a white pet crow. While he is away, Phoebus's wife has sex with a secret lover, but the crow sees everything and blabs to its master upon his return. In a fury, Phoebus kills his wife, yet when his temper cools, he realises what he's done and blames the crow. Phoebus throws the bird out and curses it, giving it black feathers instead of white, and a harsh unmusical voice, which it has kept to the present day. The story ends with a moral exhortation against the dangers of gossip.

The crow has special significance in Japan, where it was linked to the sun goddess Amaterasu. One story tells how an evil being threatened to swallow the sun, but heaven sent a crow, which flew down the monster's throat and choked it. A crow also guided the legendary first emperor of Japan, Jimmu, to find a base from which to establish his kingdom.

Old sayings

The crow has been the subject of many sayings in the past. Three interesting examples that have fallen out of fashion include:

To make the crow a pudding – to die (and so become food for crows). In *Henry V*, Shakespeare writes: 'By my troth, he'll yield the crow a pudding one of these days: the king has killed his heart.'

An evil crow, an evil egg – bad people generate bad things. Hugh Latimer used this phrase in a sermon in 1537: 'Therefore, brethren, gather you the disposition and study of the children, by the disposition and study of the fathers. Ye know this is a proverb much used: "An evil crow, an evil egg".'

Pulling a crow – arguing. In 1662, Pepys wrote in his diaries: 'At noon I dined at Sir W. Batten's, Sir John Minnes being here, and he and I very kind, but I every day expect to pull a crow with him about our lodgings.'

The most sinister aspect of the crow's supernatural connections was its association with witches. Crows are black so it is not too surprising that they are linked with creatures of the night, especially since a major component of their diet is the dead (carrion) and they have a harsh, fearsome call. Typically, a crow is said to be one of the animals that a witch can transform herself into, or the form taken by one of her 'familiars' – spirits sent out into the world to report back to her. Historically, the fear of witchcraft seemed to take a particular hold in Scotland. For example, one trial in Skye was presided over by General MacLeod of Dunvegan, who fought at the Battle of Fontenoy in 1745:

Two witches meet in this 1720 woodcut image. (*Courtesy of Wellcome Library, London*)

A woman accused of witchcraft was arraigned before him; she was condemned to be burned. Bound with cords she was laid on her back and the faggots beneath lighted with a torch. The general was present.

'Oh general,' exclaimed the victim, 'is this my reward for saving your life at Fontenoy? Do you mind [remember] a crow flying in front of your regiment?'

'Yes, Flora, I mind it well,' said the general.

'I was that crow,' said the witch, 'and kept back the balls which would have taken your life.'

Crows can be quite vocal.

'Good,' said the general; 'was the crow really you, Flora? Loose the cords and set her free instantly. The castle shall be her home, and she and hers shall never want so long as I or mine are lairds of Dunvegan.'

A fanciful tale, but the mere fact that it was published shows that a link between witches and crows was accepted, and not considered surprising. More prosaically, people in rural communities were worried about crows not because of mystic evil, but because of their perceived harm to farming: eating crops and killing immature farmyard animals. The term 'scare crow' was originally coined to describe boys who were employed to keep birds such as crows away from agricultural land. They were also termed crow boys, crow minders, crowherds or crow-keepers. Their job involved shouting or banging noisy implements all day long, as well as using a bow and arrow, a gun, or throwing stones – hence our expression 'stone the crows!' Robert Forby described the crow-keeper's role in East Anglia in 1830:

Besides lustily whooping, he carries an old gun from which he cracks a little powder, and sometimes puts in a few small stones, but seldom hits, and still seldomer kills a crow. In Shakespeare's time, it seems that the crow-keeper carried a bow, and doubtless 'handled' it with as much awkwardness and as little success as the modern boy manages his gun.

Crows at the movies

It is surprising how often crows feature in films. The most obvious example is *The Crow*, starring Brandon Lee, who was accidentally shot while filming this dark fantasy of a man brought back to life by a crow to avenge his own death. In *The Shawshank Redemption*, the prison librarian, Brooks, has a pet crow, and in a famous scene from Danny Boyle's *28 Days Later*, a crow causes Frank to become infected with the rage virus. Crows also feature prominently in *Snow White and the Huntsman*, Alfred Hitchcock's *The Birds*, and Dario Argento's disturbing *Opera*.

All of these films have quite dark themes, as befits a crow perhaps. But sometimes even crows get some light relief at the movies. Who can forget the crows that sing *When I see an elephant fly* in Disney's *Dumbo*?

Duck

Domestic duck.

*D*ucks are often portrayed as silly or amusing because of their waddling walk, endearing quacks, big bills, and the way they just seem to enjoy the water so much. This image has led to the creation of a number of humorous anthropomorphic cartoon characters including Disney's *Donald Duck*, Warner Brothers' *Daffy Duck*, the Thames Television series *Count Duckula*, and Marvel Comics' *Howard the Duck*. Long before any of these fictional avian protagonists came Beatrice's Potter's *The Tale of Jemima Puddle-Duck*. Published in 1908, Jemima is portrayed in a homely bonnet and shawl and manages to escape becoming a lunch for Mr Tod the fox, thanks to the help of friendly dogs.

The most familiar duck in the UK is the mallard, perhaps because it can adapt well to the presence of people: it is often seen in parks and on other areas of urban water. However, apart from the mallard, many other species of duck breed in this country, including the wigeon, teal, eider, shelduck and tufted duck to name a few. Whilst the word 'duck' has Anglo-Saxon roots, 'mallard' was adopted from French and derived from the term for male. Hence 'mallard' seems originally to have referred only to male ducks of this species, which was widely known until the nineteenth century simply as the 'wild duck' or 'common duck'. When brought to market the mallard was sold as whole fowl, whereas smaller species such as the wigeon and teal were called half fowl and fetched half the price.

A male mallard enjoying the water.

Domestic ducks in the UK, such as the white Aylesbury, are mostly descended from selective breeding of the mallard. However, unlike the goose, there is little or no evidence for domestication of ducks in Europe before the Romans. The Romans kept ducks, but do not seem to have especially prized them as a source of food. Until medieval times it seems likely that most ducks eaten in the UK were wild birds, as they were extremely common. Whilst the rearing and sale of domestic geese was very well developed by the medieval period in this country, duck husbandry probably only began at this time and was even then of little economic importance. The duck, like the rabbit and the eel, was sometimes regarded as food more suitable for the less well-off.

Ducks on a Roman wall fresco.

Ducks have long been hunted and many techniques were used. Ancient Egyptian wall paintings from about 1400 BC show wildfowl being brought down by hurling heavy sticks into flocks of them that had taken to the air. The Egyptians were also known to use nets. An Etruscan tomb painting from Italy created in about 500 BC shows young men bringing down waterfowl with stones from a catapult. Medieval manuscripts sometimes depict ducks pursued by hawks as part of the sport of falconry, and the riverside was known to be a popular place to pursue this hobby as other more esteemed prey, such as the heron, were also found there. However, the use of nets was the most profitable and efficient way of catching ducks, the nets being carefully laid to trap the birds in areas where they could be herded into them en masse with little chance of escape. In this manner, ducks were often taken in large numbers in the era before land drainage had removed a lot of these birds' natural habitat. An eighteenth-century account describes 31,200 ducks being taken in one season in ten groups of nets at a location in Lincolnshire, with about two-thirds of these being mallards. The development of the gun, of course, opened up new methods to kill ducks, either from shallow-draught boats or from a favourable position on land near where ducks roosted.

A woman sends her goshawk after a mallard in this scene from the fourteenth-century *Taymouth Hours*. (*Courtesy of the British Library illuminated manuscripts collection www.bl.uk*)

Ducks were also valued for their eggs and their feathers. In particular, the soft feathers of the eider duck were much sought after to make stuffed quilts called eiderdowns for the bed, as well as pillows. The down was gathered from the nests of eiders, who used hundreds of small feathers plucked from its own breast to make a soft warm repository for their eggs. The naturalist Edward Stanley explains how this was done at the beginning of the nineteenth century:

> As soon as it is observed that the first eggs are laid, they are removed, and the nests at the same time robbed of the down; and this is repeated a second or third time; but it is generally found that if they are robbed more than twice they begin to desert the place, and if pillaged oftener they quit it entirely.

Another commentator marvelled at the docility of the eider duck, which seemed so tolerant of human intervention in its intimate affairs:

> In the localities where the eider duck breeds, it is so careless, or rather so little awed by the presence of mankind, that it makes its nest not only near but among human habitations, and the female allows persons not only to take her eggs from her, but even to touch her without any timidity.

The eider duck is especially associated with St Cuthbert, a seventh-century Northumbrian saint who became a hermit on the Farne Islands. He took a liking to these birds and reared eider ducklings, tamed them, and granted them his protection so that they could not be exploited. A twelfth-century chronicler calls the eider 'the birds of the blessed Cuthbert', and they were often known in England as the Cuthbert duck or 'cuddy duck' for short.

Male eider.

Many people, like St Cuthbert, are drawn to ducklings: they are pretty, fluffy, and soon able to sustain themselves. Ducklings are also renowned for their ability to bond with a human or animal as a protector or surrogate parent. An example was reported in 1820 of a terrier bitch who lost her puppies:

> The unfortunate mother [terrier] was quite disconsolate, till she perceived the brood of ducklings which she immediately seized and carried to her lair, where she retained them, following them out and in with the greatest care, and nursing them after her own fashion, with the most affectionate anxiety. When the ducklings, following their natural instinct, went into the water, their foster-mother exhibited the utmost alarm and as soon as they returned to land she snatched them up in her mouth and ran home with them.

The dictionary writer Samuel Johnson reputedly came from a family that kept ducks and a story about this is told by John Hawkins, his close friend and biographer:

> When he was about three years old, his mother had a brood of eleven ducklings which she permitted him to call his own. It happened that in playing about, he trod on and killed one of them, upon which running to his mother, he, in great emotion, bid her write.
> 'Write, child?' said she. 'What must I write?'
> 'Why write,' answered he, so:
>
> > *Here lies good Master Duck,*
> > *That Samuel Johnson trod on,*
> > *If 't had liv'd 'twould have been good luck,*
> > *For then there'd been an odd one.*

There is a limited amount of folklore associated with ducks, although they were in various ways supposed to be able to predict a change in the weather for the worse: if they quacked particularly loudly or assembled in large numbers, for instance. Another tradition was that the colour of a duck's breastbone in autumn after cooking was a prognosticator of the harshness of the winter to come: the darker the bone the worse the winter.

A bizarre ceremony involving a duck is held at All Souls College, Oxford every 100 years. An oversized mallard is supposed to have flown out of the foundation of the college while it was being built in the fifteenth century, and was pursued through the grounds. Once every century, the college organises a hunt in pursuit of the legendary bird – at the last ceremony in 2001, the revellers chased a wooden replica duck on a pole, but in earlier centuries a real bird was employed. A 'Lord Mallard' is appointed to oversee events and a 'mallard song' is sung. English eccentricity at its best.

Ducks were also said to have certain healing properties. A seventeenth-century author describes the following 'virtues and use of the duck, and its parts':

1. A *live* duck assuages colic pains, the feathers being plucked off, and the naked part applied to the belly.
2. The *fat* heats, moistens, mollifies, digests, discusses. Therefore is of use in inward and outward pains, *viz.* of the sides and joints, in the cold distempers of the nerves, etc. Note, *this fat is preferred before all others, especially that of the wild duck.*
3. The *blood* is alexipharmacal [remedial against poisons] and hereupon is sometimes received into antidotes …
4. Its *dung* is applied to the bites of venomous beasts.

Ducks and cricket

When a batsman is out for no runs, he is said to be 'out for a duck'. This expression came about because the score of '0' is shaped rather like a duck's egg. In Victorian times the full phrase was often used. A report of a match played by cricket legend W.G. Grace in 1871 describes how 'after a duck's egg in Mr Grace's first innings, comes 200 runs in his second'. There are some variations on the basic duck theme. A batsman out first ball is said to be out for a 'golden duck' and if out without even facing a ball, this can be termed a 'diamond duck'.

Although most domestic ducks kept for their meat or eggs are descended from the wild mallard, a more recent introduction that is an exception to this rule is the distinctive Muscovy duck. This came originally from South and Central America, and is supposedly named after its musky smell. Besides laying eggs for eating, the Muscovy duck is an asset to the garden because it enjoys eating slugs. Imported duck species have also been kept for centuries as ornamental birds on lakes and ponds in parks and private gardens. Exotic varieties like the colourful mandarin duck from East Asia have been popular introductions; in Japan the monogamy of this species has been widely used in art and literature as a symbol of marital fidelity. Some of these imports have escaped captivity and have formed feral breeding populations. A notable example is the strikingly colourful red-crested pochard, which is now not uncommon on rivers and lakes in parts of England.

Fastest mallard in the world

The train engineer Sir Nigel Gresley kept ducks and when he designed one of his most famous trains – LNER class A4 number 4468 – he was inspired to call the elegant locomotive the *Mallard*. It was built in 1938 and proved to be the fastest steam train the world has ever seen: reaching speeds of over 126 mph.

The Muscovy duck (top) and red–crested pochard (below).

Eagle

Bald eagle.

*E*agles have been important symbols of strength around the world for many centuries, even in nations such as the UK where they are rare in the wild. Only two species of eagle are found on these shores: the golden eagle and the white-tailed eagle ('sea eagle' or 'erne'). Both are mainly confined to Scotland.

The eagle is often described as the 'king of birds', and the Persians were one of the earliest nations to use it as an emblem. In the fourth century BC, the military standard of King Artaxerxes II carried the image of a gold eagle with outstretched wings. It is no surprise that the Romans later adopted it as an emblem of its military might too: every legion had a standard bearing an eagle, around which the troops rallied. Many subsequent empires and nations have utilised eagles as part of their identity, including the Holy Roman Empire, Prussia, and Hitler's Third Reich. The bald eagle has been frequently used to represent the United States since its independence.

From earliest times, the Christian Church associated the eagle with St John the Evangelist, author of the fourth gospel of the New Testament. It was sometimes said that since the high-flying eagle could get closest to heaven, so St John was the closest saint to God. This is why church lecterns are often in the form of an eagle with outstretched wings: the lectern holds the Bible, and those who read it should spread the word of God and make it soar, just as St John did.

The king of the Greek gods, Zeus, was often linked with an eagle, who served him as messenger and companion. One myth suggested that this eagle was a former Greek king who had made Zeus jealous. Zeus could transform himself into an eagle too. On one occasion he did so after falling in love with the handsome prince Ganymede, and abducted him to become cup-bearer to the gods. Zeus also sent an eagle to punish Prometheus for giving the secret of fire to humans. Prometheus was chained to a rock where an eagle pecked his liver out every day; since he was immortal, the liver regenerated and the next day the eagle started all over again. This daily agony continued for centuries until the hero Hercules slew the eagle and freed Prometheus.

Perhaps because eagles were imposing, and yet were so difficult to observe in the wild, all sorts of strange tales arose concerning them. For example, a special 'eagle stone' kept in their nest was supposed to have healing powers and could for example make childbirth easier. Eagles could look at the sun without being blinded by it and were immune from being struck by lightning. Elderly eagles would make themselves youthful again by flying so high in the sky that their feathers caught fire, then plunging into cold water. It was said that dragons particularly enjoyed eating eagle eggs, which is why dragons and eagles fought so much.

Despite their powerfully majestic image, eagles were sometimes credited with less noble behaviour. In particular, there were always stories that they could carry off unattended human babies. One of the earliest examples of this is related by John of Tynemouth, best described as a fourteenth-century collector of anecdotes. He tells a tale that one day, when King Alfred was hunting in the forest, he heard the cry of an infant, which appeared to come from a tree. He sent his huntsmen searching and they climbed the tree, only to find a wondrously beautiful child in an eagle's nest at the top.

„ZUM EHRENDEN ANGEDENKEN
AN DIE TAPFEREN DEUTSCHEN KRIEGER.

The eagle of the Kingdom of Prussia (above). A church lectern in the shape of an eagle (below).

Mid–Victorian image of a golden eagle.

The baby boy was clothed in purple and had golden bracelets on his arms, demonstrating a highborn parentage. The king commanded that he should be cared for, baptised, and well educated, and in remembrance of his singular discovery, Alfred caused the boy to be named Nestingus.

A number of more recent examples of baby snatching from Scotland were described with great earnestness in the nineteenth century, all relating to events that allegedly occurred many decades before in the 1700s. The details in these stories make you want to believe them. For instance, Hannah Lamond supposedly had her baby snatched by a golden eagle while she was harvesting in Ayrshire, and was so distraught that she was driven to a death-defying climb of a steep cliff to rescue him from the eyrie, unhurt. Similarly, William Anderson and his wife were crofters on Unst in the Shetland Islands, and were amazed when a sea eagle grabbed their sleeping baby girl and carried her away across the sea to the neighbouring island of Fetlar. A rescue party there lowered a local boy, Robert Nicolson, down the cliffs on a rope to retrieve the baby and she was saved. This story has a fairy tale ending because Robert and the girl met again when adults, fell in love, and married.

The eagle was used in former times to portray important persons. When a Roman emperor died, for example, an eagle might be released as his funeral pyre burned to signify the spirit of the dead leader ascending to heaven. 'The eagle does not catch flies' is a once-popular English saying that has fallen out of use. It may originate from the fifteenth century, and means that important people don't concern themselves with trivia.

Henry II was a particularly powerful English king, who identified with eagle symbolism. He was constantly at war with various combinations of his four sons during his long reign from 1154 to 1189. A story from towards the end of the king's life is related by Gerald of Wales, and suggests a monarch wearied by family feuding:

> But it happened that there was a chamber at Winchester beautiful with various painted figures and colours, and a certain place in it which was left clear by the royal command, where a little time after the king [Henry II] ordered an eagle to be painted, and four young ones of the eagle sitting upon it, two upon the two wings, and a third upon the middle of the body, the fourth, not less than the others, sitting upon the neck, and more keenly watching the moment to peck out the eyes of its parent. But being asked by those who were on intimate terms with him what this picture might mean, he said, 'The four young ones of the eagle are my four sons, who will not cease to persecute me even unto death. The younger of them, whom I even now embrace with such tender affection, will sometime at the last insult me more grievously and more dangerously than all the others.'

And so it was to prove, for this youngest son, John – later the notorious King John – sided against his father in a final family conflict that brought a dying king to his knees. Upon hearing the news of John's involvement, the king collapsed in grief and died shortly afterwards.

White-tailed eagle (or 'sea eagle').

The eagle is an important symbol in Mexico. The Aztecs, who ruled part of the area of modern Mexico before 1521, were reputedly guided by an eagle sitting on a cactus to establish their capital city, and the eagle knights were an elite class of Aztec warrior. A golden eagle is still Mexico's national emblem and appears on its flag and coat of arms.

Eagle symbolism is significant in the UK as well. The Royal Air Force, for example, uses the emblem of an eagle. This design was adopted from a First World War forerunner to the RAF called the Royal Naval Air Service. Admiral Murray Sueter was a pioneer of military aviation in the Great War and in his book *Airmen or Noahs* gives this account of how the eagle came to be approved:

> Mr Churchill wanted an eagle for a badge to be worn on the sleeve of the coat to distinguish the naval airmen. An artist was sent for and he produced a design like a goose. But Mrs Sueter had a gold eagle brooch of French Imperial design that she had purchased in Paris. I took this eagle brooch to the Admiralty to show to Mr Churchill and Admiral Prince Louis of Battenberg. They much preferred it to the goose design of the artist and adopted it for the badge of the Royal Naval Air Service.

When the RAF was formed in 1918, the use of the Naval Air Service eagle was carried over into the new organisation.

Barclays Bank is another organisation that has always used an eagle emblem. Founder John Freame was in business as a goldsmith and banker in London by 1690. A black spreadeagle design seems to have been adopted initially, simply because seventeenth-century businesses liked to choose a distinctive picture to represent them at a time when most people could not read or write. The design has altered over the years, with a change to a blue eagle in 1970, and a move away from a traditional heraldic eagle to a more contemporary design in 1999.

Modern history: eagle vs drone

In 2016 it was reported that both the Dutch police and the French army are training eagles to identify and take drown drones operating illegally. Drones are miniature aircraft that can be used to take photos of sensitive locations such as power stations and military installations, or to carry illicit substances such as drugs. An eagle is large enough to easily disable a drone and bring it to the ground.

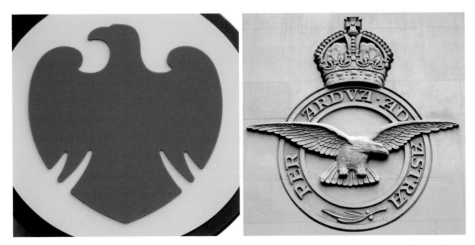

A High Street sign for Barclays Bank (left, courtesy of Barclays Bank plc) and the RAF eagle on the Bomber Command Memorial in Green Park, London (right).

Flamingo

*F*lamingos are amongst the most distinctive birds in the world: tall, with red and pink feathers, long curvy necks and large brightly coloured bill. The name is derived from the Latin word *flamma*, meaning flame, which describes the bird's bright plumage. Interestingly, the Spanish for flamingo is *flamenco*, and the same word is used to describe the vivid, passionate dance and music that is so intimately associated with this nation. The female dancers often wear red. In ancient Egypt, a picture of a flamingo was used as a hieroglyph meaning 'red'.

The association with red and flames, and the hot climates in which they live, has led some to suggest that the flamingo was one inspiration for the legend of the phoenix – the mythical bird with magical properties that was born in fire.

Flamingos were regarded as a delicacy by wealthy Romans, although eminent men could be influenced more by the kudos of the exotic origins or rarity of the food on their table than by the taste of it. A recipe for flamingo boiled in spicy date sauce has survived, but flamingo tongues seem to have been prized as an especial treat: the emperor Vitellius served a dish of them in AD 69. The birds were originally shipped over from Africa to satisfy demand, but there is a suggestion that some attempts were made in Imperial times to keep them in captivity too. The Roman poet Martial describes the birds stocked on the farm of his friend Faustinus, who lived near Naples, and one of them is assumed to be the flamingo:

Greater and lesser flamingos.

The whole muster of the farmyard roams at large: the screaming goose, the spangled peacock, the bird which derives its name from its red plumes, the spotted partridge, the speckled fowls of Numidia, and the pheasants of the impious Colchians; the proud cocks caress their Rhodian mates, and the turrets resound with the murmur of pigeons. On this side mourns the ringdove, on that the wax-coloured turtle-dove.

The emperor Caligula declared himself a living god and demanded to be worshipped, and one of the actions he insisted upon to distinguish his unique style of divinity was that rare birds such as the flamingo and the peacock were to be sacrificed daily in his honour. However, an unlucky flamingo was said to have foretold his impending assassination. While sacrificing the bird on the morning before he was killed, the flamingo's blood gushed all over Caligula's toga – a bad portent that was later interpreted as a sign that the real gods had had enough of this particular emperor.

Flamingos were familiar birds in Britain in the nineteenth century because they were widely kept in zoos and ornamental gardens. One of the most imaginative references to the flamingo in literature comes from this era. In Lewis Carroll's *Alice's Adventures in Wonderland* (1865), the young heroine describes a very unusual sport:

Alice thought she had never seen such a curious croquet-ground in her life; it was all ridges and furrows. The croquet balls were live hedgehogs, and the mallets live flamingos and the soldiers had to double themselves up and stand on their hands and feet, to make the arches. …

She went off in search of her hedgehog. The hedgehog was engaged in a fight with another hedgehog, which seemed to Alice an excellent opportunity for croqueting one of them with the other; the only difficulty was that her flamingo was gone across to the other side of the garden, where Alice could see it trying, in a helpless sort of way, to fly up into a tree. She caught the flamingo and tucked it away under her arm, that it might not escape again.

Alice with a flamingo.

Flamingos are rarely seen 'in the wild' in the UK, although occasional migrants wander up from the Mediterranean. Most are likely to be captive birds that have escaped. In the US, plastic flamingos are popular garden ornaments.

Goldfinch

*T*his bird's name is of ancient origin, so that even in Anglo-Saxon texts it was referred to as the *goldfinc*. Yet it has also been widely known for many centuries as the thistle-finch, because of its love of the seeds from that plant. Indeed, the scientific name for the goldfinch, *Carduelis carduelis*, is derived from the Latin word for thistle, *carduus*. Other common regional variants included the goldspink or gold linnet; in the Midlands its beautiful plumage led to it being known by the pleasingly appropriate name of proud-tailor.

This bird's bright plumage – especially the flashy yellow feathers on the wings – has led to an association with gold, and therefore money. Since at least Tudor times, the colloquial term for gold coins such as sovereigns or guineas was 'goldfinches', a word that was still used in the early nineteenth century. A goldfinch also became slang for a wealthy man. Hence, tradition has it that if an unmarried girl saw a goldfinch on St Valentine's Day, she would marry someone well off.

Goldfinch in art

Renaissance paintings with a religious theme often feature the goldfinch, especially works originating from Italy. The bird is frequently held by the infant Jesus or his mother, Mary. The red feathers on the goldfinch's face were said to have arisen when the bird tried to pull a thorn from Christ's head on the day of the crucifixion and was spotted with his blood. Hence in Renaissance paintings the inclusion of this bird seems to foreshadow events to come in the life of the infant. There was also a metaphor here: Christ withstood the thorns and created the Christian Church, and the goldfinch avoids harm from the thorn-like thistle and uses it to feed a family.

Goldfinches were thought to have curative powers in some European countries, perhaps because of their association with Christ, but gold too was said to be healing. Leonardo da Vinci described this belief:

> The goldfinch is a bird of which it is related that, when it is carried into the presence of a sick person, if the sick man is going to die, the bird turns away its head and never looks at him; but if the sick man is to be saved the bird never loses sight of him but is the cause of curing him of all sickness.

Goldfinches were very popular caged birds for centuries since they were beautiful and the males sang sweetly. They could also be taught ingenious tricks such as using a small bucket on a chain to draw up food and water, ringing bells, acting dead, pulling a tiny cart, and even firing a miniature cannon on command.

Some owners took to breeding their own goldfinches and a number of varieties arose such as the yellow-breasted and the white-headed goldfinches. Keepers learned that if goldfinches were raised completely in the dark or fed exclusively on hemp seed then all the colours were lost and a pure black goldfinch resulted. It was also discovered that goldfinches and canaries would interbreed to produce hybrid birds called 'mules'. These varied greatly and unpredictably in appearance: whilst some were beautiful, the majority were rather drab, although many of them seemed to have a sweet song.

Caged goldfinches live longer than wild birds. The sixteenth-century German naturalist Conrad Gesner reported one that was so elderly that its feathers had turned white with age. It was reckoned at twenty-three years old, it had lost the ability to fly and consequently stayed wherever it was placed. The bird could no longer keep itself clean, so the owner was obliged to regularly scrape its beak and claws so that it could eat, drink, and perch.

There could be unexpected consequences of keeping pet goldfinches. A gentlemen named Randal Burough from County Clare in Ireland had an unusual experience in

Examples of goldfinch and canary mules.

1836. He owned two pet goldfinches that lived in the drawing room most of the time but their cage doors were left open so they regularly flew around the house and out into the countryside. He continues the tale in his own words:

> The winter was beginning to be severe, and the food suitable for small birds consequently scarce, when one day the two goldfinches brought with them a stranger of their own species, who made bold to go into the two cages that were always left open and regale itself on the hospitality of his new friends, and then took his departure. He returned again and brought others with him, so that in a few days half a dozen of these pretty warblers were enjoying the food so bountifully provided for them. … There was soon a flock of not less than twenty visiting the apartment daily, and perfectly undisturbed by the presence of members of our family. … It was the innocent cause of making many idlers, for several strange gentlemen were in the habit of stopping for hours in amazement at the novel scene.

There was such a great demand for goldfinches as pets that they were caught in very large numbers. Even in the second half of the nineteenth century, enormous quantities were captured: around 1860, reputedly over 130,000 were taken annually in the Worthing area.

The birds were enticed towards nets using a variety of techniques: a stuffed goldfinch could be used as a decoy or lots of thistles collected together to lure them with food. A tethered tame goldfinch might be allowed to feed nearby and so attract others to join it; some bird catchers impersonated the bird's song to draw the finches closer or employed a singing caged bird to pull the wild birds in. Instead of nets, another option was to use bird lime. This was a sticky substance spread onto twigs and other perching places to which birds became stuck.

Some people objected to the abuse of wildlife in Victorian times, including author and poet Thomas Hardy, who used the goldfinch as an allegory a number of times in his writing. In *The Mayor of Casterbridge*, Elizabeth-Jane is given a caged goldfinch by her manipulative stepfather as an act of contrition for his bad behaviour towards her, but she snubs him and sends him away. The goldfinch is forgotten and is found several days later, starved to death. Upset, Elizabeth-

By the early nineteenth century, some domestic aviaries for the drawing room were large enough to accommodate flocks of goldfinches and other songbirds.

Goldfinch at the bird table.

Jane decides to forgive her stepfather, but by the time she finds him again, he too has died of starvation. Whilst the goldfinch had a physical cage, her stepfather was trapped in a cage of his own misdeeds. Hardy also wrote a poignant poem entitled *The Caged Goldfinch* suggesting, perhaps, that living creatures should not be treated as mere possessions, and that there is more to nature than simply adorning the human experience:

> *Within a churchyard, on a recent grave,*
> *I saw a little cage*
> *That jailed a goldfinch. All was silence save*
> *Its hops from stage to stage.*
>
> *There was inquiry in its wistful eye,*
> *And once it tried to sing;*
> *Of him or her who placed it there, and why,*
> *No one knew anything.*

The hunting of goldfinches reached such ridiculous proportions that the fledgling Royal Society for the Protection of Birds decided to act. One of its first ever campaigns was 'Save the Goldfinch' and fortunately, it was a great success: goldfinch trapping is now a thing of the past.

Goldfinches in recent years have flourished, and they have become a favourite in UK gardens. This means that more of us can enjoy watching them as the poet John Keats did in one of his most famous early works, *I Stood Tip-toe Upon a Little Hill* (1816). It includes these lines:

> *Sometimes goldfinches one by one will drop*
> *From low hung branches; little space they stop;*
> *But sip, and twitter, and their feathers sleek;*
> *Then off at once, as in a wanton freak:*
> *Or perhaps, to show their black, and golden wings*
> *Pausing upon their yellow flutterings.*

Birds of a feather

Over the centuries, wordsmiths have coined appealing terms to describe assemblages of certain birds. A notable example is a *charm* of goldfinches, which seems to originate from the Anglo-Saxon *cirm*, meaning chatter or noise, especially from many voices together. The phrase 'a chyrme of fynches' dates back to at least the early fifteenth century. This example, and a number of other collective nouns for birds, evoke the sound made by gatherings of a particular species, and include an *exaltation* of larks, a *gaggle* of geese, and a *murmuration* of starlings.

Other collective nouns reflect the perceived behaviour of a bird. Owls are believed to be intelligent, so their assembling is described as a *parliament*, suggesting some sort of wise council. Teals are small ducks that leap into the air when they take off; hence a collection of them is known as a *spring*. A *murder* of crows recalls the potentially sinister overtones of such a gathering, given this bird's customary association with death or evil.

There have been modern attempts to add to these long-standing terms, with suggestions such as a *scold* of jays or a *screech* of gulls, but they have not been widely adopted.

Goose

Canada geese.

*T*here are seven or so species of wild goose that are commonly seen in the UK, although there are other less frequently seen species. The most familiar are the Canada goose and the greylag goose, and the winter visitors are the barnacle and the brent goose.

The ancient Egyptians kept various species of goose in captivity for food, but also as sacrificial offerings to the gods. The goose was especially dedicated to Geb, lord of the earth and the underworld, and the father of Isis. European domesticated geese are derived particularly from the greylag, which was formerly known as the 'wild goose'. The white feathered varieties which now predominate as farmyard geese are the result of selective breeding in captivity over a period of hundreds of years. The Romans described white geese, and medieval bestiaries from the UK noted that a proportion of domestic geese were white, although many contemporary illustrations show them having a similar colouration to their wild ancestors.

Geese were a source of food, and throughout Europe, domestic geese were herded on foot to fairs for many centuries – from ancient Rome to medieval Britain. In the 1850s, there were flocks of domestic geese in Lincolnshire of up to 10,000 birds. There are still three historically established 'goose fairs' that operate in England, the most famous being Nottingham Goose Fair, which has its origins in the reign of Edward I in the thirteenth century. Annual goose fairs were often held around the time of Michaelmas (29 September), which honoured 'St Michael and all the angels', and when it was traditional to eat a roast goose – a practice that dates back to at least the fourteenth century. A popular saying was: 'If you eat goose on Michaelmas Day you will never want money all the year round.' Apart from the meat of the goose, the eggs were also eaten, and goose fat had a wide variety of uses in medicines, cooking, and as a lubricant. The goose's liver was, and still is, prized as a delicacy when force-fed a special diet to enlarge it.

The usefulness of the goose did not end there. Before the invention of the pen, the only implement used for writing in ink was the quill – usually plucked from the wing of a goose. However, a fresh feather was too soft to use. To prepare the feather for life as a writing tool, it had first to be dressed so that it would have a reasonable longevity; amongst other processes, this involved hardening the end of the shaft by passing it through hot ashes or plunging into boiling water. The soft down feathers of the goose were widely used for stuffing pillows, cushions, mattresses and so forth, and these were typically harvested from live birds every two months from March until autumn. These feathers were plucked from under the neck, the wings, and from the breast.

In ancient Rome, a flock of geese sacred to the goddess Juno, wife of Jupiter, was credited with preventing the fall of the city. In 390 BC, Rome had been invaded by the Gauls. The people fled, but a small defiant garrison remained atop the rocky Capitoline Hill. The Gauls besieged the garrison, and one night stealthily scaled the edifice, one by one, without alerting the Roman guards or their dogs. However, the sacred geese in Juno's temple sensed something was amiss and they hissed, cackled, and beat their wings to wake the Roman garrison commander, Marcus Manlius, who raced out and started

The wild greylag goose (above) and domestic white 'farmyard' geese (below).

propelling Gauls over the cliff edge. His soldiers came running to help and the garrison was saved; eventually the garrison and the ruined remnants of Rome were liberated without the Romans ever having completely abandoned their city. Over 450 years later, Pliny explained that the highest ranking magistrate in Rome, the censor, still always personally ensured that Juno's geese were well fed.

Improbable chimney sweeps

Geese are well known for 'getting in a flap' when they are afraid or feel threatened. A cruel countryside practice in times gone by, still occasionally referred to in the second half of the nineteenth century, was to drag a live goose on a rope up a chimney by its feet. The manic beating of wings dislodged the soot.

There was an extraordinary belief about the barnacle goose in Europe, which has been written about in the UK since at least the twelfth century. Even as late as the seventeenth century, educated people seriously believed that barnacle geese were not hatched from eggs – indeed, they were unable to lay them. Instead, the view was that these geese were born from a variety of barnacle that either grew on trees overlooking the sea or were carried into the oceans on pieces of drifting wood. A species of barnacle, still called the goose barnacle, sometimes found washed ashore on timbers, does look superficially like a tiny goose. In 1635, John Swan, a clergyman and doctor, explained how all this took place:

Early thirteenth-century depiction of the barnacle goose tree. (*Courtesy of the British Library illuminated manuscripts collection www.bl.uk*)

> In the north parts of Scotland and in the islands adjacent called Orchades [Orkneys], are certain trees found, whereon there groweth a certain kind of shell-fish of a white colour, but somewhat tending to a russet, wherein are contained little living creatures. For in time of maturitie the shells do open and out of them, by little and little, grow those living creatures, which falling into the water when they drop out of their shells, do become fowls such as we call barnacles or brant geese. But the other that fall upon the land perish and come to nothing.

Barnacle geese and brent geese have some superficial similarities so they were often credited as being varieties of the same species. They are also both migratory birds that only come to the UK during the winter, so residents of these islands never saw them breed – hence the great mystery of how they reproduced and the fact that no one ever saw their eggs.

Another mystery is the figure of Mother Goose, the fabled originator of many tales including nursery rhymes such as *Sing a Song for Sixpence*. We may never know who created her, or if she was based on a real person, but she is first mentioned in writing in the mid-1600s. Mother Goose began to acquire a clearer physical identity when she became the subject of a popular new pantomime in London in 1806 called *Harlequin and Mother Goose*. A patronising review at the conclusion of that season at Theatre Royal Covent Garden gave this verdict:

> A most successful season, which … is principally to be ascribed to Mother Goose, who without depending on any play, drew profitable houses for ninety-two nights. That a goose should be able to do so much for a theatre must be very flattering and encouraging to many of our dramatists! … It has, however, been thought, and by no bad judges, that this attendance on 'Mother Goose' is an impeachment of the taste and common sense of the public, but whatever it may prove, it is clear, from the song, that it is very natural, for 'birds of a feather will flock together'.

The spite and snobbery for which the acting industry has become renowned is clearly not a modern phenomenon! One of the most celebrated performers of the part of Mother Goose in panto was the actor and comedian Dan Leno, who defined the character when he played it at Drury Lane in 1902–1903. The story usually involves a pantomime dame who gives up her beloved goose to a demon who promises to make her beautiful, but she gradually realises that looks matter less than the simple affection between herself and her pet, and she fights to get the goose back.

One of the most common species of wild geese seen in the UK today is the Canada goose. However, it was not originally native to the UK and comes from North America. The first recorded appearance here was when Charles II installed some in his ornamental gardens, now St James's Park, in London. Other landowners copied

The actor Dan Leno as Mother Goose at Drury Lane in 1902.

the king, and by the eighteenth century enough birds had escaped to establish a resident population. These birds do extremely well in the UK climate and are more ready to live and breed in areas close to people than other varieties of goose. Nowadays a new species of 'foreign' goose is mastering the same trick. The Egyptian goose, from Africa, once only found as ornamental birds in parks and gardens, has established a large breeding population in the UK, although mainly confined to east and south-east England at the present time.

Goose sayings

There are a number of old sayings involving geese that have survived into modern English, such as sending someone on a wild goose chase, getting goose bumps, or 'he wouldn't say boo to a goose!' However, geese were such a prominent feature of life in times gone by that many more such phrases existed including these:

- The old woman is plucking her goose. (It's snowing.)
- All his geese are swans. (He always exaggerates.)
- Such a reason my goose pissed. (Said if anyone offered an unlikely explanation for something.)
- Shoeing a goose. (Wasting time on a pointless exercise.)
- I care no more for it than a goose turd for the Thames. (I don't like it much.)
- You'll be good when the goose pisseth. (Geese don't urinate, so I'm not expecting a change.)

Egyptian goose.

Grebe

Great crested grebe.

On water, the grebes are elegant and sophisticated swimmers, but on land they are clumsy waddlers, and this has earned them the wonderfully appropriate regional name of 'arsefoot'. There are two main species found in the UK: the great crested grebe and the little grebe.

The great crested grebe undergoes significant changes in plumage throughout its life – it is striped when immature, has a beautiful black and orange head crest in the breeding season, and is pale and crestless in the winter. Some of our ancestors were confused by this and assumed these plumages represented different species. The great crested grebe has had various regional names including the car goose, gaunt, and horned ducker.

The chest, belly and flanks of the great crested grebe are covered with a densely packed, lustrous, warm down and the skins were formerly employed in the clothing industry. So-called 'grebe cloth' or 'grebe fur' was used to make muffs and the trimmings to hoods or sleeves known as tippets. In fact, so widespread was this usage that alternative names for the great crested grebe in the nineteenth century included 'satin grebe' and 'tippet grebe'. The demands for the birds' skins were such that the great crested grebe was hunted mercilessly and their numbers plummeted to dangerously low levels.

A group of women realised that the slaughter of wild birds such as the grebe simply to support ladies' fashions was unacceptable and they formed an action group in 1889: The Fur, Fin and Feather Folk. Their members pledged not to wear feathers if they came from birds that had been killed solely for this purpose. Within a year the group

Little grebe.

had thousands of members and they and other similar groups began to exert significant pressures on clothing sales and conservation, which ultimately led to the great crested grebe being saved as a British breeding bird. In 1891, this powerful action group merged with the Society for the Protection of Birds, which acquired the approval of the monarch in 1904 and became the Royal Society for the Protection of Birds or RSPB.

The little grebe is a rare example of a British bird that is still widely known by an alternative name – the dabchick. Why this alternative name has persisted is unclear, particularly since the bird has a wealth of regional names including dive-dapper, divy duck, dopper and Jack Doucker. It is quite a shy bird, but this can be seen as an endearing characteristic. Writers across the centuries have noted that when disturbed it silently disappears beneath the water 'as if by magic' and then hangs low in the water until the coast is clear. Shakespeare captures the grebe's behaviour in his play *Venus and Adonis*; the handsome young man is coaxed reluctantly into courtship by the goddess after she makes a vow to him:

> Upon this promise did he raise his chin
> Like a dive-dapper peering through a wave
> Who, being look'd on, ducks as quickly in.

The Aldbourne dabchicks

The residents of Aldbourne in Wiltshire have traditionally been known as 'dabchicks', a practice that may date back to before the seventeenth century. The story goes that an unfamiliar small bird once visited the village pond, but no one knew what it was. An old woman announced it was a dabchick and the villagers, presumably pleased that they had something unusual in their midst, began to use the word as a kind of community nickname.

Sixteenth-century image of the little grebe or dabchick.

Gull

Kittiwake.

Given that gulls are such common birds, it is perhaps surprising that they are associated with a limited amount of folklore. Gulls did not do much to draw our ancestors' attention – they didn't sing, were not beautiful, did not make attractive pets, and they weren't a pest that devoured crops. Adult gulls were not generally eaten either, because they tasted unpleasantly tough and fishy. However, in the seventeenth century, Robert Plot described black-headed gulls that bred in large numbers every year at an inland pool on the estate of Sir Charles Skrymsher in Staffordshire. The immature gulls tasted much better than the adults and were eagerly rounded up for the table:

> After three weeks sitting [on the nest], the young ones are hatched, and about a month after are almost ready to fly, which usually happens on the third of June, when the proprietor of the pool orders them to be driven and catched, the gentry coming in from all parts to see the sport.

They were sold for five shillings per dozen, but even at this cheap price so many birds were captured that sometimes Sir Charles made a quite substantial windfall:

> Some years the profit of them has amounted to fifty or threescore pounds, besides what the generous proprietor usually presents his relations and the nobility and gentry of the county withal – which he constantly does in a plentiful manner,

Black-headed gull.

sending them to their houses in crates alive, so that feeding them with livers and other entrails of beasts they may kill them at what distance of time they please, according as occasions present themselves, they being accounted a good dish at the most plentiful tables.

In other areas, gulls' nests were raided for their eggs, and the birds were also killed for their feathers to stuff pillows and so forth. Adult gulls were occasionally eaten by shipwreck survivors when nothing else was available, and people living on remote islands might also consume them – but where possible, other sea birds such as puffins, fulmars and gannets were preferred on grounds of taste.

Gulls take more than a year to reach sexual maturity and the plumage of young birds is often very different to the mature adult. This caused much confusion in the minds of people from earlier centuries who believed that adults and immatures were entirely different birds. For example, even at the beginning of the nineteenth century, many contemporary books described a bird called the 'wagel' as a separate species, whereas it is actually the juvenile of either the herring gull or other larger gulls; similarly, the so-called 'brown gull' and 'red-legged gull' were names erroneously given to immature black-headed gulls. Furthermore, since the black-headed gull only has its black head

Immature gulls like this herring gull are brownish, leading many naturalists in the past to conclude they were a separate species called the wagel.

in the summer, naturalists believed that the summer birds and the winter birds were completely different creatures.

The delightfully named 'kittiwake' is another example of a species of gull whose young were once mistakenly believed to be a different species – being known as the tarrock. The word 'kittiwake' is imitative of the characteristic cry of this bird, and the word 'gull' itself might have a similar origin in the sound that gulls make. It may be derived from Celtic languages, perhaps originally meaning something like weep or wail in reference to the gull's call. The modern Welsh word for gull is *gwylan* and there are similar words in other Celtic languages such as Cornish and Breton. The Anglo-Saxon name was *meau* from which came the terms 'mew' and 'maw', both used to describe gulls in the past. Byron uses mew in his poem *Childe Harold's Pilgrimage* (1819), when describing the main protagonist's departure from England by ship:

Adieu, adieu! my native shore
Fades o'er the waters blue;
The night-winds sigh, the breakers roar,
And shrieks the wild sea-mew.
Yon sun that sets upon the sea
We follow in his flight;
Farewell awhile to him and thee,
My native land – good night!

The seagull on stage

Anton Chekhov's play *The Seagull* is one of his four major works. The pointless shooting of a gull by the character Konstantin is a central event in the play, but the life of the gull becomes in part an allegory for the lives of both Konstantin and Nina, with whom he is in love. Accordingly, the play ends with Konstantin, the gull-killer, shooting himself.

For centuries, the most widely held belief about gulls was that they were the wandering souls of sailors lost at sea, so seafarers have traditionally been careful not to injure them. A story told in parts of Wales tells how Dylan, a sea god, becomes jealous of an old man and his three beautiful daughters. He creates a big storm, and a large wave rises up and sweeps the girls away to keep him company beneath the sea. But when he sees the father's grief, Dylan is instantly filled with remorse and turns the daughters into gulls so that they can continue to accompany their father whenever he walks by the sea.

Another persistent tale is that the behaviour of gulls can be used to forecast a change in the weather. When gulls leave the sea and flock inland this is said to be a sign of an impending storm, hence the traditional rhyme: *seagull, seagull, sitting on the sand; it's never good weather when you're on the land*. This conviction was even upheld in official circles in Victorian times. Robert Fitzroy, who has been dubbed the Father of Meteorology,

Skating on thin ice – the black-headed gull lacks its black head in winter plumage so our ancestors thought it was a different bird.

was a forecaster employed by the Royal Navy. In his *Weather Book*, published in 1857, he wrote:

> When sea-birds fly out early, and far to seaward, moderate wind and fair weather may be expected. When they hang about the land, or over it, sometimes flying inland, expect a strong wind with stormy weather.

There is some logic to this belief, in that the developing sea swell and other changes as a storm approaches tend to drive fish from the surface so that gulls may be more inclined to seek food on land instead. Many gulls, of course, commonly derive their sustenance from the land anyway, rather than the sea or shore. This fact is particularly commemorated by the Mormons or Latter-day Saints in the US. When their leader, Brigham Young, led them into what is now Salt lake City, Utah in 1848, their first crops were attacked by hordes of insects. Fortunately, thousands of gulls came to the rescue and ate the insects, which saved the crops and thus ensured the survival of the fledgling community. A large monument was erected to this 'Miracle of the Gulls' and one species – the California gull – was consequently adopted as the state bird of Utah.

Gulls do not commonly have associations with other religions, although one sixth-century Christian saint does have a particular connection. Cenydd was a crippled Welsh prince who was abandoned as a baby because he was the product of an incestuous relationship. His cradle was swept out to sea, where a flock of gulls spied him; they guided the boat ashore and dragged him out. Determined that he should survive, the birds tore out their feathers to make a bed for the infant prince, and protected him from the elements with their wings; a deer suckled him with her milk, and an angel gave him protection and educated him. When he grew up he became a celebrated holy man who lived as a hermit, founding the church at Llangennith on the Gower Peninsula; his name is sometimes anglicised to 'St Kenneth'.

Gulls and U-boats

U-boats sank thousands of British merchant ships during the First World War.

The Admiralty and the British government were desperate to tackle the U-boat menace in the First World War. If left unchecked, German submarines would impose such a stranglehold on imports of food and vital supplies, that Britain might be forced to capitulate. Since there was so much at stake, the authorities considered many schemes to counter the threat.

Bizarre as it may now seem, one proposal was to use gulls to detect U-boats. The idea was that dummy U-boats should be towed behind ships releasing meat to train wild gulls to associate them with food. Soon, it was suggested, hungry gulls would flock to any raised periscope and so reveal its position. A wealthy businessman, Thomas Mills, became the main proponent and even patented a submarine-shaped automated training apparatus for the gulls. He became obsessed that his plan would 'win the war' but the Admiralty, wisely, disagreed and never trialled the scheme.

The Germans had more success with their own gull initiative. Their most effective surface-operating ship of the Great War was the *Möwe* ('the gull'), which operated as a fast-attack raider, sinking forty British ships during the conflict.

Heron

Grey heron.

Our ancient ancestors saw the heron as an enigmatic creature with supernatural powers. The Egyptians of the New Kingdom, for example, worshipped a bird god called Benu, often portrayed as a heron, who was linked to creation and rebirth. It was the harsh cry of Benu that marked the beginning of time and which would one day mark its end. Interestingly, the Romans also had myths that linked the heron to the generation of new life. The poet Ovid explains that the heron came into being after a town to the south of Rome, called Ardea, was ransacked by the Trojan hero Aeneas. All the buildings were burned to the ground, but out of the smoking ruins arose a tall, pale bird that shook the town's grey ashes from its wings and then first uttered its mournful cry. In fact the scientific name for the grey heron found in Britain and Europe is still *Ardea cinerea*, which means 'the ash-coloured heron'. Roman prophets, known as augurs, regarded the appearance of herons as a good omen.

The vernacular name of 'heron' – and, until the nineteenth century, 'herne' – has roots in Norman French. This is not surprising because it was the language of the nobility after 1066 and medieval nobles enjoyed hunting herons. The words that they used to describe their favoured pursuits were consequently foisted on the conquered Anglo-Saxons and eventually adopted into what is now English. The unfortunate herons were attacked with birds of prey such as the peregrine, gyrfalcon and goshawk. This popular pastime, known as heron-hawking, is even mentioned by Chaucer in *The Canterbury Tales*. However, in the wild, birds of prey do not usually attack the adult heron – it is far larger than their natural quarry – so they had to be trained to do it. This was done by introducing them to herons raised in captivity with meat attached to them; hence these hawks, or 'heroners', came to associate the sight of the heron with food.

Egyptian bird-god, Benu. (*Courtesy of Jeff Dahl, kindly shared via Creative Commons and GNU Free Documentation License, Version 1.2*)

Parties of hunters with trained birds of prey would journey to places where herons were known to live, and release their birds to hunt. An influential thirteenth-century discourse on heron-hawking by Holy Roman Emperor Frederick II described the sport in detail. He recommended that two falcons were more effective than one to bring down a heron, and advocated the use of a hunting dog to retrieve the dead quarry. A hunt might take some time, but observers would follow their birds on horseback in order to watch the action. Despite its obvious cruelty, the heron was considered the most noble of the falconer's quarry, and in its heyday was very popular amongst persons of wealth. However, heron-hawking had largely died out before the nineteenth century: its last refuge was Didlington Hall, Norfolk, where it was finally abandoned in the late 1830s.

During hawking, the heron occasionally eluded its attackers, but the birds were so high in the sky that onlookers often could not see how the heron had escaped. This led

Heron hawking in the seventeenth century.

to curious explanations. English theologian John Shaw described one prevailing belief in 1635:

> [The heron] hath her nest in very loftie trees, and showeth as it were a naturall hatred against the gossehawk and other kinde of hawks; and so likewise doth the hawk seek her destruction continually. When they fight above in the aire, they labour both especially for this one thing: that the one might ascend and be above the other. Now if the hawk getteth the upper place, he overthroweth and vanquisheth the heron with a marvellous earnest flight; but if the heron get above the hawk, then with his dung he defileth the hawk and so destroyeth him: for his dung is a poyson to the hawk, rotting and putrifying his feathers.

There were other peculiar ideas about the heron. As late as the nineteenth century, it was supposed that the heron's bodyweight waxed and waned with the moon: the bird being fattest at full moon. The fat from a heron killed at full moon was used to treat rheumatic pains, perhaps because people observed the bird's indifference to the cold and wet, which is often said to bring these pains on. Given the heron's sharp vision, its fat was claimed to improve eyesight, and it was also poured into the ears to relieve deafness. Rubbed onto fishing rods before putting them away for the winter, heron fat acted 'as a preservative alike for damp or dryness'. The heron's skill at catching fish was believed to be at least partly due to the miraculous powers of its feet, which somehow had the power to attract its prey, perhaps by a special scent. This curiously persistent myth led to anglers soaking their bait or fishing lines in water containing herons' feet in the hope of making it irresistible to fish.

An unusual pet

Herons were occasionally taken as pets, but this was generally only successful if the bird was captured before it fledged. Irish ornithologist Robert Warren raised a heron that he took from a nest in 1847, but not without difficulty:

> The bird is much attached to me, as I always feed it, runs towards me shaking its wings and keeping up a cry evidently of pleasure. It evinces much gentleness of disposition, and frequently stands caressing me with its bill. But to strangers its manners are very different, as it attacks them with the greatest fury, and although repeatedly driven back will continue to return to the charge.

The heron terrified his dogs, sending them running away yelping, and in a long-running dispute with Warren's cockerel, the heron emerged victorious every time.

A heron waits patiently for a catch.

The heron was once commonly eaten by the great and powerful. At the feast held for the installation of George Neville as Archbishop of York in 1465, the list of provisions describes 400 herons being consumed. The bird seems to have been a delicacy enjoyed by the wealthy since they were expensive to obtain and had royal protection. A law passed during the reign of Henry VII forbade herons to be taken except by hawking or the longbow, and since at least Tudor times, destruction of a heron's eggs attracted a fine. An early seventeenth-century law prevented use of a gun within 600 paces of a heron nesting site. Some landowners built or tended to a heronry on their land to maintain local stocks for hunting and eating. However, the consumption of herons gradually fell from fashion amongst the wealthy. Perhaps the last recorded occasion in which herons were eaten at a formal public banquet was recorded in 1812, at the Hall of the Stationers' Company in London, when the assembled diners tucked into six herons along with thirty-two lamb's tongues, 40 stones of beef, twenty-four marrow bones, forty-six capons, thirty-two geese, four pheasants, twelve godwits, twenty-four rabbits and other fare.

Yet herons continued to be shot for private eating in some parts of the country until at least the closing years of the nineteenth century. Opinion, however, seems divided on the bird's taste. Some found the flesh unpleasantly fishy, while others compared it favourably to meats such as hare or goose. The solution to this apparent contradiction may lie in the manner of preparation for cooking: heavy seasoning and use of spices was often recommended. Fifteenth-century cookbooks recommended cooking the bird with bacon and ginger or pepper to obtain the best taste. A seventeenth-century recipe for heron pie advises preparing each bird as follows:

> Break the breast-bone of the heron, parboyl it in water and salt, shred sweet herbs with onyons, and make them up into little balls, with butter, put them into the belly, and season it with pepper, salt and nutmeg.

Apart from their fat and their flesh, herons were also killed for their feathers. After a successful hunting by hawks, the long black plumes of the heron's crest were much prized and it was a privilege to be awarded them. Medieval knights and lords often wore them in their caps or helmets and, indeed, the ceremonial dress of the Most Noble Order of the Garter, founded in 1348, still includes a black velvet cap adorned with white ostrich feathers and black heron plumes.

The bicycle bird

A heron logo has long been associated with the Raleigh Bicycle Company. There is a myth that this bird was adopted when Raleigh built their new factory in Nottingham in the 1930s because it was located in a watery part of the city where herons were common. However, the origins of the company's bird emblem are older than this. The business was founded by Frank Bowden after he bought a small bicycle manufacturer that had a workshop in Raleigh Street, hence the company name. The Bowden family crest consisted of a heron's head and his firm officially adopted it in 1908. The distinction of being able to use the family's crest was heightened when Frank Bowden was granted a baronetcy in 1915.

The Raleigh logo. (*Courtesy Raleigh UK Ltd*)

Jackdaw

Originally this bird was called simply the daw – a name that was probably imitative of its call. The prefix 'jack' may have been added as an endearment, in a similar manner to Tom Tit or Maggie Pie (magpie). Jonathan Swift seems to endorse this explanation in his poem *Salamander* (1705):

> *As mastiff dogs, in modern phrase, are*
> *Call'd Pompey, Scipio, and Caesar;*
> *As pies and daws are often styl'd*
> *With Christian nicknames, like a child*

People from all walks of life were familiar with jackdaws. They were confiding, cheeky, even thievish when food was around, and the name Jack was customarily associated with a certain boldness of character: Jack Frost, Jack-a-napes, Jack the Giant Killer, little Jack Horner and so forth. The jackdaw's popularity is borne out by many contemporary descriptions that reveal a fondness for the bird's personality and behaviour. For example, Edward Stanley, Bishop of Norwich, wrote a widely read book about birds in 1838:

> The habits of a jackdaw are known to everybody; wherever found, he is the same active, bustling, cheerful, noisy fellow. Whether in the depth of a shady wood remote from cities and from towns, or whether established in the nooks and niches of some Gothic cathedral tower in the very midst of the world, it matters not to him. He seems to know neither care nor sorrow – ever satisfied – always happy! Who ever saw or heard of a moping, melancholy jackdaw?

An alternative – or maybe complementary – theory for the bird's name suggests that instead of being purely an endearing sobriquet, the title 'jack' was chosen because it was sometimes taken to mean 'little' in the past. Jackdaws, of course, are small members of the crow family.

Jackdaws have a varied diet and so were easy and cheap to keep as pets; they could occasionally be taught to say a few words or whistle a tune, and contemporary accounts often note these birds' loyalty to their owners. The author Jane Roberts wrote an account of a voyage to Australia and back in the 1830s and describes a pet jackdaw called 'Jones' that the captain's wife kept on board. He had a cage, but was very sociable and was allowed the freedom of the ship while at sea, to the delight of passengers and crew:

The bustling, busy jackdaw.

Jones was the cleverest and most amusing bird possible: he whistled certain tunes, which he repeated on the deck and on the poop, and then came to inspect and interfere with everything in the cuddy ['saloon']. … At dinner he was generally one of the party, going from plate to plate for what he wanted. Sometimes, indeed, he attempted to help himself without leave, and then he was scolded, but in a tone of voice to give encouragement rather than reproof.

As Roberts describes, jackdaws are sociable birds. In the wild, they live together in communities and even in ancient times, this was remarked upon. The Greek philosopher Aristotle refers to a contemporary proverb that noted, 'Similar persons are friends; whence also it is said: "like tends to like; a jackdaw to a jackdaw".' This has the same meaning as our more modern phrase 'birds of a feather flock together'. Jackdaws like to nest together on cliffs and in tree holes, but have readily adapted to the niches in manmade environments that occur on tall buildings such as churches. This seems to be a longstanding relationship: for many centuries they were reported as nesting atop the lofty sarsens of Stonehenge.

Jackdaws have a well-known propensity for making their homes in chimneys and towers, but their nests of dry sticks can be a fire risk. For example, the conflagration in 1816 that destroyed Shanes Castle, seat of the O'Neill family in Antrim, was reputed to have been caused by jackdaw nests in the chimney catching fire. York Minster was ravaged by a fire in 1840, caused by a careless clockmaker who left a candle burning, but contemporary commentators attributed the rapid spread of the blaze to the many jackdaw nests in the tower where the fire started.

Jackdaws like to nest and roost in chimney pots.

There is a limited amount of superstition associated with the jackdaw. Perhaps the most persistent story is that sighting a solitary jackdaw is bad luck – a rather uncommon event given the jackdaw's gregarious nature. In the eleventh century, William of Malmesbury told the tale of a woman who heard a jackdaw chattering, and predicted it heralded great ill fortune. Apparently it did, because she soon learned that many of her family had died in an accident. Workmen in Bristol reacted with dismay when a lone jackdaw sat on a chain spanning the river Avon during the construction of the Clifton Suspension Bridge; shortly afterwards, one of them was seriously injured in an accident. A jackdaw falling down your chimney has been considered particularly likely to spell ill fortune.

Clever birds

Like the crow, the jackdaw has been regarded as an intelligent bird. The seventeenth-century ornithologist Francis Willughby notes, 'The head of this bird, in respect of its body, is great, which argues him to be ingenious and crafty: which is found true by experience.' Many owners of tame jackdaws noted their bird's ability to recognise individuals or to learn from experience.

Scientific support for this behaviour came from Cambridge University in 2015. A researcher wore a particular mask whenever she approached jackdaw nests to weigh their chicks – a behaviour that the parent birds understandably found threatening. The scientist wore a different mask if she was just walking by. The parent birds rapidly learned to attend their nests more quickly if a researcher appeared wearing the 'chick-weighing' mask than the 'walking past' mask, demonstrating an ability to recognise individual human faces.

Jay

*T*he scientific name for the jay is rather charming and reflects well-known aspects of this bird's behaviour: *Garrulus glandarius* means the 'chattering lover of acorns'. In fact, its liking for acorns is such that the jay will on occasion hoard or bury them, in the same way that squirrels do. One late November day, I watched a jay return again and again to the tube of an old firework that had been left standing upright in the garden. At each visit he dropped an acorn in, before flying away to get another, and the jay continued until the tube was full. The bird's habit of hiding acorns is well known, and was even described by Aristotle. It is one method by which new oaks are brought into existence and, somewhat romantically, it has been suggested that jays are the souls of Britain's ancient druids, who are still tending to their sacred trees.

In the wild, the jay has a harsh call that has often inspired regional names. It was called the 'scold' or 'Devil scritch' in Somerset, for example, and in Welsh it was *screch y coed* – screamer of the wood. The authors of medieval bestiaries liked to draw comparisons between animals and desirable or undesirable human qualities, and the jay's abrasive voice meant it was invariably compared to gossips and slanderers. The *Aberdeen Bestiary* was compiled in about 1200 and declares:

Eighteenth-century woodcut image of a jay.

> The jay lives in the woods and flies chattering from one tree to another, as a talkative man ceaselessly tells others about his neighbours, even the shameful things he knows about them.

A handsome bird, the jay was commonly kept as a pet by our ancestors: either in a large cage or as a 'chamber bird' that was permitted to roam parts of the house. Some were even allowed to fly free and accompany an owner on walks, since they could be trained to come when called. But the jay's extraordinary ability to mimic attracted particular attention: various writers describe it impersonating other birds such as the greenfinch, buzzard, or owl with uncanny accuracy, but also animals such as a lamb bleating or the bark of a dog. In Thomas Bewick's *History of British Birds* (1797), the author recalls two rather unusual examples:

> We have heard one imitate the sound made by the action of a saw so exactly, that though it was on a Sunday, we could hardly be persuaded that the person who kept it had not a carpenter at work in the house. Another, at the approach of cattle, had learned to hound a cur dog upon them, by whistling and calling upon him by name.

Edward Jesse, surveyor of the royal parks, related an amusing anecdote in 1834 regarding a lawyer in Somerset who kept a jay. This bird was an admirable mimic: he imitated chickens, ducks, and the neighing of a horse so convincingly that household staff were frequently deceived. However, he also impersonated one of his owner's employees:

> A clerk of this attorney had a very singular laugh, and when laughing he used to put up his shoulders, and raise his eyebrows and hair, in a manner that may be best understood by attempting the same thing. It is a fact that this bird not only imitated with success the clerk's laugh, but used also, at the same time, to raise the feathers of his head in imitation of the clerk's hair. This he did whenever he had a bird's eye view of the young man, to his great annoyance, and to the infinite amusement of those who were present.

Jays could also be taught to remember a short tune played on a musical instrument, and even to say a few words. A pet jay's ability to speak fascinated people, and was recorded as early as the twelfth century. It was so well known by the time that Geoffrey Chaucer wrote *The Canterbury Tales*, that he could compare the jay to more unlikely avian vocalists:

> *Now had this Phoebus in his house a crow*
> *Which in a cage he fostered many a day,*
> *And taught it to speak, as men do teach a jay.*

Hand-coloured mid-Victorian picture of the jay.

Unfortunately, despite these endearing qualities, wild jays have been heavily persecuted over the past 500 years. Under a Tudor law, the jay was identified as 'vermin' to be hunted out and destroyed: each dead jay attracted a payment of one penny from the churchwardens of a parish. This Act of Parliament was not repealed until the mid-1700s. Jays were held responsible for eating crops – particularly cherries and peas – and were included on most gamekeepers' lists of culprits blamed for stealing the eggs of game birds such as the pheasant and partridge. Dead jays were left strung up on country estates along with rats, magpies, foxes, and a long list of others – 'a beautiful addition to the usual list of malefactors', as one saddened Victorian writer put it.

The jay's fine-looking plumage makes it unmistakable – a mixture of pink, blue, black and white – but this beauty, coupled with the bird's raucous voice, means that its name has been used in English to describe a showy or 'flash' person. For example, Imogen in Shakespeare's *Cymbeline*, says: 'Some jay of Italy … hath betray'd him.' In the eighteenth century and into the Victorian era, the jay's attractive blue wing feathers were eagerly sought by makers of women's hats, so this became another reason to kill them. The feathers were also much prized by fly fishermen to make their lures – in about 1750, angler Richard Bowlker said his 'shorn' fly made from jay feathers never failed: 'This is as killing a fly as ever I know.'

Getting married?

Jays are not usually gregarious, and are typically encountered only in ones or twos. However, in spring they will sometimes congregate, in what are known as 'jay marriages', to find a mate. Here is Thomas Bewick's description of this noisy event:

> They sometimes assemble in great numbers early in the spring, and seem to hold a conference, probably for the purpose of pairing and of fixing upon the districts they are to occupy. To hear them is truly curious: while some gabble, shout, or whistle, others with a raucous voice seem to command attention. The noise made on these occasions may be aptly compared to that of a distant meeting of disorderly drunken persons.

Kingfisher

On account of its great skill at catching prey and its majestic plumage, this bird was literally the king of fishers, a title used since at least the 1400s. Our ancestors admired the beauty of the kingfisher, but such a strikingly handsome bird was so out of the ordinary that it's no surprise that it had its own unique creation myths. The ancient Greeks told the tale of a very happily married couple – Alcyone ['al-sy-an-ee') and Ceyx ['see-ix']. They were very much in love, but Ceyx had to go to sea, and unfortunately his ship was wrecked in a storm. Morpheus, the god of dreams, came to Alcyone in her sleep and told her what had happened and, grief-stricken, she awoke and threw herself into the sea to drown. The gods were so moved by the couple's love for each other, that they brought them back to life as beautiful kingfishers that were destined always to live together beside the water. The plaintive call of the birds was said to echo Alcyone's grief and sorrow, and the Greeks' name for the kingfisher became the halcyon in her memory.

Another legend relates that the kingfisher was originally a drab little bird that Noah released from the ark with instructions to look for land. The bird was so thrilled to be free after weeks of being shut away that he flew up and up into the sunny cloudless sky, enjoying his liberty. Yet he flew so high that some of the sky's blue colour rubbed off on him, and as he went higher still, turning over to enjoy the warmth, the sun singed his chest and belly feathers orange. He revelled in his freedom for hours, until eventually he realised that he had forgotten his mission and went back to search for the ark, but he was lost and never managed to find it again. To this day, the kingfisher sits watching the

A kingfisher depicted in Conrad Gessner's *Historia Animalium* (1554).

water hoping to catch a glimpse of the ark, before flying off, racing desperately up and down the waterways to continue his hunt for Noah. It's a delightful story.

The Greeks and the Romans wrote about the kingfisher's significant influence over the weather. Few people had seen the kingfisher's well-hidden riverside nest, so the belief arose that it bred at sea during the winter but needed calm waters to do so. Distinguished ancient writers such as Aristotle described the bird's floating nest, and Pliny explains that it was protected by Aeolus, heaven's keeper of the winds and the father of Alcyone. Aeolus 'imprisons the winds and forbids their roaming' for fourteen days – the so-called Halcyon Days, during which time all kingfishers were supposed to build their nests at sea and hatch their young unmolested by storms. These were the winter days when sailors could safely set sail. The phrase 'halcyon days' is still sometimes used when recalling a short period of peace and contentment from the past.

This myth led to another strange conviction about the kingfisher. As late as 1853, the Reverend John Wood recounted that it was still widely accepted that a kingfisher's corpse could be used to forecast the weather:

> In many parts of the country it is fully believed that if a kingfisher is dried and suspended by the beak, the breast will always turn in the direction of the wind. This belief has caused the death of no few kingfishers, whose suspended bodies may be seen in many a cottage, their brilliant blue and red plumage rotating in a most impartial manner.

The playwright Christopher Marlowe refers to this belief in *The Jew of Malta*, written in about 1590:

> *But now how stands the wind?*
> *Into what corner peers my Halcion's bill?*

The seventeenth-century polymath Sir Thomas Browne was so vexed by this irrational belief that he set up a series of experiments to disprove the meteorological skills of the deceased kingfisher. He suspended two dead ones on strings, side by side, and observed them once they had each stopped swinging; they ended up, of course, pointing in totally different directions even when hanging inside a glass jar. He published this refutation, but it did not seem to stop people believing otherwise.

But the bird's perceived magical properties did not stop here. A dead one in the house was claimed to stop the building being struck by lightning. In the eighteenth century, the dried heart of the kingfisher was described as preventing epileptic fits when hung around the necks of children, and if you were lucky enough to find the floating nest of the kingfisher it was a cure for leprosy sores and certain eye conditions. However, the most bizarre account of the kingfisher's powers is to be found in a rather fantastical book. Published in 1658, *The Magick of Kirani and of Harpocration* claims to be based upon twelfth-century Latin translations of much older works by a former king of Persia

The little fisherman waits …

and an ancient Greek. Whether this is true or not, the book was eagerly digested by a population fascinated by magic and mysterious cures:

> If anyone ties the eyes of this bird in a cloth, and lay them at the head of one that sleeps too much, they will keep him from sleeping. If any shall carry its eyes when he sails at sea, he shall not fear tempest nor storm, nor any necessity whatever. Also the pilot that carries them shall steer his vessel quietly and without the affliction of a storm. And its heart carried, will make a man beautiful and loved and endeared, and peaceful to all people; though a man fall into the midst of his enemies he shall receive no harm, and he shall neither be hurt by storm nor thunder; but he shall be acceptable and peaceable to all. … And if a fisher[man] carry the belly or the head or the feathers, that fisher[man] shall never be disappointed. And the whole bird roasted in its feathers and eaten, quiets people possessed with the Devil. And set in the house, it averts all sedition and strife.

Unfortunately, very large numbers of kingfishers were shot in the nineteenth century. They were killed because of the alleged magical properties of their corpses, for stuffing as ornaments, to produce lures for fly-fishing, and to stop them predating on immature fish in trout streams. They were also shot by sportsmen for entertainment, and by so-called ornithologists who wished to examine them: a bird 'sighting' by many gentlemen naturalists in the nineteenth century often meant a miss with both barrels.

Sadly, kingfishers were popular stuffed birds in Victorian times.

Life after death?

In 1187, the chronicler Gerald of Wales described prevailing beliefs about the kingfisher, which he called the martinet because some people said that it nested on St Martin's Day:

> It is remarkable in these little birds that if they are preserved in a dry place when dead, they never decay; and if they are put among clothes and other articles they preserve them from the moth and give them a pleasant odour.
>
> What is still more wonderful, if, when dead, they are hung up by their beaks in a dry situation, they change their plumage every year as if restored to life – as though the vital spark still survived and vegetated through some mysterious remains of its energy.

Did the plumage rejuvenate by magic?

Kite

*T*he name 'kite' dates back to Anglo-Saxon times, originating from the Old English name for the bird, *cýta*. It was also formerly widely known as the glede, especially in northern England, a word derived from the Anglo-Saxon *glida*, to glide, which reflects its graceful method of flying.

The species endemic to Britain is the red kite, but it is known across Europe: the ancient Greeks were so familiar with it that the bird appears in no less than five of Aesop's Fables, including this one:

The Hawk, the Kite, and the Pigeons

The pigeons, terrified by the appearance of a kite, called upon the hawk to defend them. He at once consented. When they had admitted him into the cote, they found that he made more havoc and slew a larger number of them in one day than the kite could pounce upon in a whole year.

Moral: Avoid a remedy that is worse than the disease.

Pliny notes that the kite was a bird whose behaviour was studied by Roman augurs in order to predict the future: 'Kites do not normally drink, and it is a direful omen if one does so.' However, he also notes, 'Though they are rapacious birds and are always hungry, they do not steal food at funerals or when it has been offered to the gods.' Despite its magnificent appearance, the red kite was never trained for hawking. It was deficient in speed and, as Aesop hints in the fable above, it was not aggressive enough. In fact, the Roman name for the kite was *milvus*, which medieval writers believed was derived from the Latin phrase *mollis avis* ('docile bird').

In medieval and Tudor times, bestiaries and allegorical publications imparted moral instruction using short memorable stories. Aesop's fables were well known, but many other authors penned their own versions. The Italian writer Laurentius Abstemius wrote a collection published in 1495, which was widely read. He includes this cautionary tale:

A Mouse and a Kite

A simple mouse had the fortune to be near at hand when a kite was taken in a net. The kite begged of her to try if she could help her out. The mouse gnawed a hole in it and set her at liberty, and the kite ate up the mouse for her pains.

Moral: Save a thief from the gallows and he'll cut your throat.

At the time of Henry VIII, the kite was a common sight in London, being apparently attracted to the offal and other waste generated by butchers and poulterers. Indeed, their role in removing this offensive material and other carrion was considered so valuable that they were granted royal protection. The kites became accustomed to people and were often seen scavenging amongst the crowds on busy streets. Kites were also one of the birds commonly noted at gibbets, feeding off the remains of people who had been executed.

The kite was very common in Shakespeare's time and he makes numerous references to the bird in his plays. In *Coriolanus* he describes London as 'the city of kites and crows'. The fact that the kite often derived its sustenance from carrion earned it a somewhat ignoble reputation compared to, say, the peregrine that fearlessly hunted for live prey. Shakespeare and other writers exploited this comparison, using the term 'kite' as an insult. King Lear, for example, rounds on his villainous daughter, Goneril, with the insult: 'Detested kite!'

The kite's tendency to simply snatch domestic birds for food caused aggravation. As far back as 1523, Sir Anthony Fitzherbert wrote of the importance of keeping chickens away from the kite 'and other vermin'. The ornithologist Francis Willughby described the kite with despair in 1678:

They are very noisome [harmful] to tame birds, especially chickens, ducklings and goslings; among which, espying one far from shelter, or that is carelessly separated

Late eighteenth-century portrayal of a red kite.

a good distance from the rest … they single it out and fly round, round, for a while marking it. Then of a sudden dart down as swift as lightning, and catch it up before it is aware – the Dam [lady of the house] in vain crying out, and men with hooting and stones scaring them away. Yea, so bold are they, that they affect to prey in cities and places frequented by men; so that the very gardens, and courts, or yards of houses are not secure from their ravine. For which cause our good housewives are very angry with them, and of all birds hate and curse them most.

To rid themselves of the bird's predations, people trapped the kite with sticky lime twigs, and used nets, and snares. At the beginning of the nineteenth century, kites were still noted as 'not uncommon' in England. They were familiar enough for Sir Walter Scott to use this delightful phrase in the *Fair Maid of Perth* in 1828: 'her ear for bad news was as sharp as a kite's scent for carrion.' However, kites were by then being persecuted wholeheartedly by farmers and gamekeepers because they took poultry and game birds such as pheasants. The use of firearms meant that far greater numbers of kites could be destroyed. By the 1850s, the ornithologist Francis Morris considered it a marvel that any kites still survived and expressed fears for their extinction in the UK. By 1881, an article in the London *Standard* noted that the kite was 'almost extinct'.

By the 1930s, there were probably fewer than ten breeding pairs of red kites in the bird's last precarious refuge, mid-Wales. A sustained protection plan there, coupled with a programme of re-introduction in the rest of the UK from the late twentieth century onwards, has seen the kite population escalate remarkably.

Modern history: the kites of Reading

Scientists were mystified that so many red kites were seen in the town of Reading in Berkshire. Modern towns do not offer anything like the same amount of carrion for the kite as medieval settlements, and yet kites haunted Reading in large numbers. An investigation published in 2014 revealed the reason: many residents enjoyed the beauty of the kite so much that over 4,000 households regularly left raw meat in their gardens to feed them.

Lapwing

Our ancestors who worked the land were very familiar with the lapwing because it favours freshly ploughed fields. It was also common in open areas such as damp meadows and pasture where livestock might be taken to graze. The lapwing is a distinctive bird that has acquired a particularly wide range of regional names. Many of these attempt to imitate the lapwing's unique, plaintive call, and examples include the peewit, weep, phillipene, and tewit. The well-known alternative name of 'green plover' is a description of the bird's handsome plumage, yet a host of other regional names seem quite obscure such as hornywink, toppyup and wallop. The name 'old maid' may be a reference to the tale from some parts of Europe that lapwings were the spirits of spinsters wandering the world still looking for husbands.

The word 'lapwing' might sound relatively modern but its origins are, in fact, very ancient and can be traced back to at least the eleventh century. The word comes from the Old English *hléapewince,* meaning 'leap and totter', a delightfully expressive reference to the bird's rather unsteady looking manner of flight. The later regional names of 'flopwing' and 'flap-jack' have arisen from the same observation.

Lapwings were commonly eaten in the past. They were so numerous and were easily caught with nets or nooses, sometimes using worms as bait to lure them close. Their eggs were taken as well and sold in enormous numbers since they were considered a seasonal delicacy. When the breeding season began in spring, rural communities would rush to look for the valuable nests, and this behaviour may have inspired the traditional Easter egg hunt. In some parts of England, dogs were trained to sniff out lapwing eggs and in the spring they patrolled areas where the birds nested. The dogs would stand and 'point' at nests until the collector came up and could gather the 'plover eggs' into their baskets.

The great egg mystery

'Where do all the plovers' eggs come from?' asked Charles Dickens in a magazine article in 1869. They turned up in enormous quantities in the spring to be eaten at dinner, lunch, weddings, balls and parties and were especially sought after in London. 'Prodigiously good they are,' he observed enthusiastically, 'but prodigiously mysterious also.' His conundrum was that although there seemed to be huge numbers of eggs for sale, a casual walk in the countryside showed that there were no longer huge numbers of lapwings.

Many of the genuine lapwing eggs came from remote areas of eastern England and Scotland, and even from Holland. But part of the answer to Dickens's question also seems to be that other birds' eggs were frequently substituted for the much-prized lapwing egg – black-headed gulls particularly, but also redshanks, godwits, even rooks.

Lapwing egg.

Strangely, despite its beauty and the fact that it was such a useful bird economically, the lapwing was widely viewed not as a blessing, but as a sinful creature. This may be one reason why our ancestors had little compunction in killing them and persistently raiding their nests.

If lapwings perceive that their nest or chicks are threatened, they use every art to distract or intimidate an intruder: low swooping dives aimed at the offender, incessant clamouring calls, and they will even feign an injury such as a broken wing to lure a predator away or stand some way away and call the raider to them. These diverting behaviours, far from being admired by our ancestors, led to the bird's reputation for deceit. In his *Parliament of Fowls*, Geoffrey Chaucer condemned the bird: 'The false lapwing – full of treacherie.' Similarly, in Shakespeare's *Measure for Measure*, the character of Lucio says:

> … 'tis my familiar sin
> With maids to seem the lapwing and to jest,
> Tongue far from heart.

There is a myth that the lapwing was present at the crucifixion and mocked Christ, and it's lamenting call has supposed to be expressing regret for this ever since. A folk tale originating in Sweden recounts how the lapwing was a former maid of the Virgin Mary,

Lapwing resting.

but she stole a pair of scissors from her mistress. As punishment the maid was turned into a lapwing and condemned to tell the world of her crime forever, uttering the call 'tyvit! tyvit!', meaning 'I stole them! I stole them!'

At one time, lapwings were known as 'ungrateful birds' in Scotland because they came north of the border to breed, but then returned to England with their young to feed the old enemy. Yet there was an additional reason for unpopularity in parts of Scotland: the lapwings' loud calls were asserted to have frequently given away the haunts of groups of Covenanters. This persecuted group often met in secret open-air places to discuss the defence of their Presbyterian beliefs and the authorities were all too pleased with any informers who helped to track them down – avian or human. The Scottish poet John Leyden evokes the scene of Covenanters fleeing both the authorities and the lapwings:

> The lapwing's clamorous whoop attends their flight,
> Pursues their steps where'er the wanderers go,
> Till the shrill scream betrays them to the foe.

The call of lapwings, particularly at night, was held to be an ill omen in parts of the English midlands, where it was claimed to resemble the word 'bewitched!'. In Leicestershire, the sound of The Seven Whistlers was believed to herald death or a catastrophe such as a mining disaster, and this story may have its origins in the eerie call of the lapwings. Miners would refuse to go down the pit the next day if they heard the sound. The birds were said to contain the souls of Jews who had assisted at the crucifixion and were condemned to float in the air forever.

Saving the wounded warrior

Not all folklore associated with the lapwing casts it as treacherous. One ancient Lincolnshire dynasty, the Tyrwhitts, trace their family name and coat of arms (three lapwings) from an old story that the founder of the lineage, wounded in battle, was only saved by the constant crying of some disturbed lapwings that showed his followers where he lay seriously injured.

Regardless of the several reasons advanced for not favouring the lapwing, they were put to good use on many private estates. The ornithologist Francis Orpen Morris noted in 1850: 'They are often kept in gardens, where they are very serviceable in devouring insects, and at the same time ornamental.' Eighteenth-century natural history writer Thomas Bewick relates the story of a lapwing kept for this purpose by the Reverend Joseph Carlyle, vicar of Newcastle:

Two of these birds, given to Mr Carlyle, were put into a garden, where one of them soon died; the other continued to pick up such food as the place afforded, till winter deprived it of its usual supply. Necessity soon compelled it to draw nearer the house, by which it gradually became familiarised to occasional interruptions from the family. At length one of the servants, when she had occasion to go into the back-kitchen with a light, observed that the lapwing always uttered his cry 'pee-wit' to obtain admittance. He soon grew more familiar; as the winter advanced, he approached as far as the kitchen, but with much caution, as that part of the house was generally occupied by a dog and a cat, whose friendship the lapwing at length conciliated so entirely that it was his

Eighteenth-century portrayal of a lapwing.

regular custom to resort to the fireside as soon as it grew dark, and spend the evening and night with his two associates, sitting close by them and partaking of the comforts of a warm fireside. As soon as spring appeared, he left off coming to the house and betook himself to the garden; but on the approach of winter, he had recourse to his old shelter and his old friends, who received him very cordially. Security was productive of insolence; what was first obtained with caution, was afterwards taken without reserve: he frequently amused himself with washing in the bowl which was set for the dog to drink out of, and while he was thus employed he showed marks of the greatest indignation if either of his companions presumed to interrupt him.

Ostrich

Male ostrich.

*T*he largest of living birds, the ungainly looking ostrich has fascinated people because of its size, strength, behaviour and speed. In many ways, it is surprising that human exploitation did not result in the extinction of the ostrich. Many other large flightless birds such as the dodo, the giant moa, and the great auk were slaughtered mercilessly by our ancestors until there were none left. However, the ostrich may owe its survival in part to the fact that it is not like the slow and unsuspecting dodo and great auk; it is a wary bird with a very fast turn of speed. It can also inhabit very remote areas.

The ostrich was an important animal to native peoples living in Africa, and is commonly depicted in the rock art of African bushmen dating back thousands of years. Some of the earliest known examples of human artwork are patterns scratched onto fragments of ostrich egg shell. The shells are hard like porcelain and so are quite durable, and they may have been used for drinking, carrying or storing water. Some coloured and engraved ostrich egg fragments from southern Africa date to about 60,000 BC, but more recent examples that are merely a few millennia old have been found in many countries including Iraq, Spain, Egypt and Greece. The use of eggshells to make jewellery is also an ancient practice. The ostrich shells are cut into small rounded pieces and a hole bored in each; they can then be strung together to form necklaces and bracelets.

Ancient Namibian rock art depicting an ostrich (left). African villager working ostrich egg fragments to create a necklace (right).

The ostrich's big feathers help to protect the bird from the sun, but humans have valued them as fashion accessories for thousands of years. They are large, fluffy and eye-catching, yet durable. These feathers were worn by horses that pulled the chariots of Egyptian pharaohs, they formed the fans used by Assyrian kings, and the plumes on the helmets of Roman generals. In the afterlife, the Egyptian goddess of justice, Ma'at, wore an ostrich feather headdress and weighed a person's heart against a large feather to determine whether they had lived a virtuous life. This feather is often assumed to be an ostrich feather.

In Europe, ostriches became popular animals to keep in menageries. They were exotic and unusual, and could live a long time if well treated. People were fascinated by all aspects of the bird and its behaviour, but a recurring theme is the voracious appetite of the ostrich, which makes it eat almost anything. Indeed, in Victorian times a person who would eat almost anything put in front of them was said to have 'the stomach of an ostrich'. Numerous reports describe the amazement of those who dissected captive ostriches after death to ascertain the cause of their demise. This report comes from John Warwick of the Surrey Zoological Gardens in 1832:

> On opening an ostrich that died at Exeter Exchange after being some years in the possession of Mr Cross, there were found besides a large quantity of rubbish, a handful of buttons, nails, marbles, stones, several keys, the brass handle of a door,

The ostrich's small-sized head in proportion to its body may have contributed to its reputation for not being intelligent.

a copper extinguisher, a sailor's knife, a butcher's hook, an iron comb, with penny pieces and coins to the amount of 3s 4½d; and besides these various articles, there were several cowries [and] glass beads, such as are used for the purposes of trade traffic by the natives of the Barbary Coast whence the bird was brought.

A medieval myth persisted into the seventeenth century that ostriches liked to eat iron. This curious belief seems to have its origins in the description of the birds given by the Roman author Pliny, who noted that ostriches have a great appetite and will eat and digest almost anything. The erroneous fable about ostriches digesting iron was so persistent that the birds were frequently portrayed in medieval bestiaries and bibles holding horseshoes in their beaks. The Tudor poet John Skelton writes these lines in his *Book of Phillip Sparrow*:

> The ostrich that will eat
> A horseshoe so great,
> in the stead of meat …

Shakespeare also picks up this theme in *Henry VI, Part 2*. The rebel leader, Jack Cade, threatens the Sheriff of Kent with the words:

> I'll make thee eat iron like an ostrich, and swallow
> my sword like a great pin, ere thou and I part.

An ill-fated ostrich was presented by the Moroccan Ambassador to the Dutch people as a gift in 1659. It was exhibited in Amsterdam, where many people came to see it and

Scene from the St Mary Psalter (c.1310) showing a man feeding horseshoes and nails to an ostrich. (*Courtesy of the British Library illuminated manuscripts collection www.bl.uk*)

eagerly threw iron nails to the bird, which it promptly ate. When the bird died a few days later, the post-mortem revealed about eighty nails in the poor ostrich's stomach. This story is often mistakenly associated with a bird kept in the Tower of London's Royal Menagerie; an ostrich did die there after eating iron, but it choked on a single 'large nail that stopped its passage' in the 1750s. This was probably another attempt to test the popular theory that ostriches loved iron.

Prince of Wales's feathers

The traditional emblem of the male heir to the British throne is three white ostrich feathers arising from a gold coronet with the German motto *Ich dien* ('I serve'). It is widely used to represent the prince and certain Welsh institutions, and is perhaps most familiar as the reverse of a former design of the two pence coin. This origin of the badge is generally traced back to Edward, the Black Prince (1330–76), the eldest son of Edward III, who probably inherited the emblem from his mother. A romantic tale that the prince adopted the feathers from the gallant King of Bohemia, killed at the Battle of Crécy, is not true.

Prince of Wales ostrich feathers on the two pence coin.

Ostriches were often allowed to roam free in Victorian zoological gardens, where their appetites led them to 'frequently astonish the visitor by suddenly snatching out of his hand a bun or cake'. They commonly stole and swallowed a remarkable array of items, and there are many accounts in Victorian literature of bizarre objects being found in the stomachs of ostriches that died in captivity. Fascinated investigators reported finding items such as a snuff box, an intact chicken's egg, a parasol handle, the remains of a mop head, pieces of glass, buttons, cutlery, parts of a lantern, and broken china amongst much else.

Unsurprisingly, many of these swallowed items were declared to have killed the ostrich concerned, and this behaviour added to its reputation for being 'stupid'. The ostrich has a very small head for its size, which caused people to think that the bird could not be intelligent, but there was also that curiously persistent story of ostriches burying their heads in the sand. They did it, so it was said, on the basis that if an ostrich couldn't see you, it felt it had somehow become invisible. The story is completely fabricated, but it probably started with an account by the Roman naturalist Pliny, who stated that ostriches will foolishly thrust their head into a bush and assume that no one can see them.

Over the centuries, ostriches have been exploited for their meat, leather, and their body fat, which was said to have medicinal properties. However, historically, it was their feathers that attracted the most interest. Ostrich plumes had already become fashionable amongst the wealthy upper echelons of UK society by the early years of the nineteenth century. At George III's Grand Fete in Windsor in 1805, a journalist described the ladies present: 'ostrich feathers to the number of eight or nine were universally worn and diamonds in profusion.' By the middle of the century, ostrich feathers had become more affordable and were an essential raw material for European ladies' attire. Centres of fashion such as Paris, London and New York imported huge numbers of them, and ostrich plumes were highly prized. They decorated hats, were used to make fans and long scarf-like feather boas, formed a notable decoration for parasols, and were employed as showy elements of dresses and brooches. Old black and white photographs of fashionable ladies from the past do not necessarily do the feathers justice, as many of them were dyed bright colours. Black ostrich feathers were considered an appropriately sombre decoration for horses and carriages at Victorian funerals.

Although the plumes originally came from wild birds, ostriches soon began to be farmed in South Africa in the nineteenth century. Here the tame birds could be plucked from time to time to feed the plumage trade, and kept in captivity while they grew more. It is perhaps no surprise, therefore, that new uses for the feathers originated in South Africa: the first ostrich feather duster was invented there in 1903 by Harry S. Beckner, who initially tied the feathers to a handle to help clean the machinery in his broom factory.

The enthusiasm for feathers in the fashion industry continued right up until the First World War, but the beginning of hostilities signalled the sudden death of the ostrich plumage trade. The austerity of wartime and restrictions on imports meant that clothing became simpler and more functional; luxury fashion items or ostentatious clothing was both unaffordable and inappropriate for the times. A large and highly profitable industry plummeted to insignificance almost overnight. There was a short-lived revival of interest in the twenties, but it was insufficient to restore the ostrich feather to anything like its prominence in the nineteenth and early twentieth centuries.

There was another resurgence in interest in ostrich products in about the 1970s. Ostrich farming began to become commercially viable, with birds being reared

Ostrich feather hat, boa, and fan.

Three female ostriches.

principally for the meat, which was advertised as being particularly low in fat. Other products included ostrich leather, feathers, and eggs. South Africa still leads the world in ostrich farming, but it has also been taken up in other countries such as Zimbabwe, Australia, and the US.

Ostrich racing

These birds can run faster than a horse and will bear the weight of a small man. Hence ostrich races were and are popular in parts of Africa and, more recently, the US. The birds are hard to control and require special saddles and reins. Surprisingly, ostrich racing was also staged regularly in London at Batty's Hippodrome in Kensington during the early 1850s. According to one reporter, the birds 'really seemed to enjoy the sport as much as any of the spectators'.

Ostrich race rider.

Owl

Barn owl.

Our ancestors were suspicious of the crow because it was black, the colour of darkness, but the owl's obvious associations with night-time provoked even more anxiety. I was on holiday in Africa in 2015, and was delighted to spot a rare species of owl hiding in the crevice of a tree. Our local guide, however, was not impressed and refused to come with me to see the bird. 'They are unlucky,' he said, 'people say they bring death'. This is how many of our European ancestors would have reacted. Night-time was when the ungodly ventured forth – witches, spirits and the supernatural – and yet this was the owl's time to be active. It was silent on the wing, secretive, inhabited lonely places such as ruins, and saw everything with its large eyes: maybe even reporting its observations to the powers of darkness. On top of all this, there was that eerie hoot or screech, of course. No wonder people were frightened of them.

The human fascination with owls is longstanding: owls appear amongst the animals depicted in French prehistoric cave paintings dating to around 30,000 BC. Other birds are rarely depicted.

To the Romans, owls were birds that presaged disaster and death. One was said to have perched on top of the senate house and hooted to foretell the death of the emperor Augustus, for example, and an owl was claimed to have prophesied the death of many other important men. Roman historian Pliny noted that an owl seen in towns or anywhere in daylight was a dire portent that often heralded death. One was seen in the build-up to the Battle of Carrhae in 53 BC and, despite having a far larger army, the Romans suffered one of the most ignominious defeats in their history at the hands of the Parthians. Aware of Roman superstition about owls, Shakespeare makes use of it in his play *Julius Caesar*, where Casca tells Cicero about the portents heralding Caesar's assassination:

An owl being mobbed by other birds from a thirteenth-century bestiary. (*Courtesy of the British Library illuminated manuscripts collection www.bl.uk*)

> And yesterday the bird of night did sit
> Even at noon-day upon the market-place,
> Hooting and shrieking.

The owl's ominous nature even seems to alarm other birds who will 'mob' an owl that they find sleeping in daylight and chase it away. This was a popular image of the bird, and Shakespeare makes reference to this and other attributes of owls in his plays. In *Henry VI, Part 3*, for example, the king exclaims that an owl must have appeared at the birth of the wicked Duke of Gloucester – a well-known ill omen: 'The owl shriek'd at thy birth, an evil sign.' Undeterred, Gloucester promptly displays the aforementioned evil and kills the king. In *Macbeth*, the owl is poetically dubbed 'the fatal bellman, Which gives the stern'st good-night'.

The owl's ability to cause or prophesy disaster is cited by Chaucer, who calls it a prophet 'of woe and of mischance', and numerous other early British writers pick up the same theme. Hearing an owl when indoors presaged a death in the household, and if you were very unlucky the owl might sit on the roof or even look in at you through the window. Shakespeare's contemporary, Edmund Spenser, has these lines in his epic *Faerie Queene*:

> *The messenger of death, the ghastly owle,*
> *With drery shriekes did also her bewray.*

The owl's association with death is found in other cultures outside Europe too, from China to India, and also Africa, as already noted. In the UK, the barn owl attracted particular dread in the past, probably because of its white, ghostlike appearance and its unearthly calls. Its unique look and habits have earned it many other names including screech owl, hissing owl, white owl, and church owl. The last of these arose because of its habit of nesting in church towers. Its peculiar screams and hisses can be quite unnerving if heard when out alone at night, something that the naturalist Gilbert White wrote to a friend about in 1773:

Sixteenth-century image of a little owl.

The white owl does indeed snore and hiss in a tremendous manner; and these menaces well-answer the intention of intimidating; for I have known a whole village up in arms on such an occasion, imagining the churchyard to be full of goblins and spectres. White owls also often scream horribly as they fly along; from this screaming probably arose the common people's imaginary species of screech owl, which they superstitiously think attends the windows of dying persons.

The two commonest species of owls in the UK are the tawny owl, known in the past as the brown owl, and the little owl. The latter was only a very rare visitor until being introduced into England in greater numbers from Europe in Victorian times.

Medieval Christians often used the natural world as a metaphor, to illustrate for the populace how they should, and should not, behave. Some early writers portrayed the owl, for example, as signifying those who had fled the light of God and given themselves up to the dark world of sinfulness. There is also a traditional Christian tale involving the owl. In this story, Christ visits a baker and asks for some bread. The baker obliges and prepares to bake for him, but his daughter is irritated that her father has set aside such a large loaf and she takes away half the dough. Yet when the loaf is baked it turns out to be much larger than expected. 'Ooh, ooh, ooh!' she exclaims in surprise, and as Christ takes it from her he turns her into an owl because of her meanness, and she still utters that expression of surprise even to this day. This tale was very well known in Shakespeare's day, and it explains an apparently random remark made by Ophelia during her mental breakdown in *Hamlet*: 'They say the owl was a baker's daughter.'

Owls were regarded as enchanted creatures and a widespread custom was that dead ones afforded protection to a building. In particular, farmers commonly killed an owl and nailed it to a barn door to avoid the evil eye and safeguard against disasters such as being struck by lightning. Owls were also frequently exterminated by farmers and keepers because they were believed to eat immature game birds, pigeons, and farmyard fowl. The magical properties of the owl extended to its curative use as well. Owls' eggs were said to counteract drunkenness and to stop someone turning into an alcoholic; but there were stranger medicinal uses, including the centuries-old remedy known as 'owl broth'. One correspondent to a newspaper recorded its use as late as 1863:

HOOPING-COUGH – A gentleman whom I met the other day at a dinner party in the country, told me that in some parts of Yorkshire 'owl broth' is considered a specific [cure]; and that he had shot these birds several times at the request of cottagers, in order that they might be able to prepare it for children afflicted with hooping-cough.

W.J. Bernhard Smith, Temple.

However, the screech owl could apparently harm children as well as save them – behaviour that clergyman John Swan reported with scepticism in 1635:

Some (in old time) have fabled strange things to this bird, namely that it sucked out the blood of infants lying in their cradles, and with the very eyes of it did assassinate children, or change their favours.

Despite the bird's sinister reputation and its resulting persecution, it wasn't all bad news for the owl. The followers of Genghis Khan, for example, venerated the owl because one was credited with saving the life of their leader. The story goes that at some point

Tawny owl.

in the twelfth century, Genghis hid from his enemies in woodland. An owl alighted on a branch just above him and his foes, afraid of the bird and also reasoning that Genghis couldn't be hiding where a wild bird perched, passed on without finding him. Genghis duly escaped.

One culture valued the owl above all others, and in complete contradiction to most of the rest of Europe, prized these birds for their intelligence and as bringers of good fortune. The ancient Greeks esteemed the owl as the emblem of Athena, the goddess of wisdom and war. It is a small tribute to the influence of this ancient civilization that their positive image of this bird is now the one that we recognise today – the 'wise old owl', rather than the harbinger of death and disaster. Athena was the patron of the city of Athens, to which she gave her name, so owls were particularly associated with that city. In fact, live owls and owl ornamentation were so widely used in Athens, that the phrase 'sending owls to Athens' became a proverb signifying a pointless act, rather like our 'carrying coals to Newcastle'. The Athenians even used owls on their coinage.

The Greeks regarded even the sight of an owl as a good omen. When General Themistocles was preparing for the naval battle of Salamis in 480 BC, an owl flew over the Greek fleet and may even have landed on his ship. This was taken as a good sign and the Greeks were decisively victorious against the Persians. At least one Greek general took owls with him to release before battle to hearten his men.

The owl and the nightingale

Maybe the most famous fictional owls are Harry Potter's pet snowy owl called *Hedwig* in the books written by J.K. Rowling, and the owl in Edward Lear's *The Owl and the Pussycat* verse. However, real life is often stranger than fiction and the story of one tame owl and its famous owner ought to be better known.

In 1850, Florence Nightingale was in Greece and rescued an owlet from the torments of local children. She adopted the little owl, whom she called Athena, and trained her to perform tricks such as bowing to guests. The nurse allowed Athena to sleep in her room at night and, somewhat eccentrically, she carried the owl around in her apron pocket during the day. The owl proved to be a devoted companion for five years, but unfortunately the story has an unhappy ending. The Lady of the Lamp left Athena in the care of family while she prepared to go to the Crimea. They forgot about little Athena and she starved to death in the attic. However, Miss Nightingale never forgot her beloved owl and in the true spirit of Victorian England she had Athena stuffed and put in a glass case.

Florence Nightingale and her owl.
(*Courtesy of Wellcome Library, London*)

Parrot

Alexandrine parakeet.

*T*here are over 390 species of parrots, including parakeets, macaws, and cockatoos. They are thought of as intelligent birds that can learn phrases of human speech, tunes, and tricks. This, coupled with their often bright plumage, has made them popular pets over the centuries. Parrots can also live a very long time; the record breaker is believed to be a sulphur-crested cockatoo called Cocky Bennet from Australia who was 119 years of age when he died. Even though he was virtually featherless for his last two decades, Cocky maintained a constant stream of banter in the bar where he saw out the last third of his life. Stock phrases included 'One at a time gentlemen please!' and 'If I had another bloody feather I'd fly!'

For his first seventy-eight years, Cocky had been the pet of a Captain Ellis who operated ships in the South Seas. Parrots seem to have long been popular pets for mariners – some Royal Navy vessels are known to have had them since at least the nineteenth century. In 1872, it is recorded that HMS *Volage*, for example, had a parrot named Laura who was allowed the freedom of the main deck when in port. Yet parrots on board can pose problems. In 2005, HMS *Lancaster*'s parrot, called Sunny, repeatedly embarrassed senior officers by shouting out 'arse' and 'bollocks'. On one occasion she was even locked in a broom cupboard when top brass arrived to inspect the ship, but she could still be heard. Fortunately, Sunny was more ladylike when she met the Queen and Prince Philip.

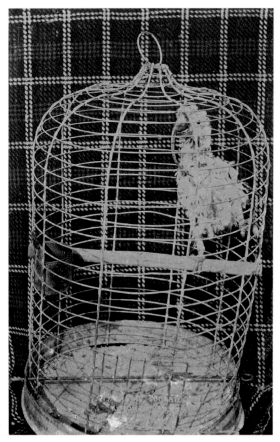

Before the era of *Pirates of the Caribbean*, the classic portrayal of the pirate was a man with one leg and a parrot on his shoulder. This image was popularised by Robert Louis Stephenson in his book *Treasure Island*, where Long John Silver has a parrot called Captain Flint. Here is Long John explaining something of the history of his bird to the book's hero, young Jim Hawkins:

'Here's Cap'n Flint – I calls my parrot Cap'n Flint, after the famous buccaneer – here's Cap'n Flint predicting success to our v'yage. Wasn't you, cap'n?'

And the parrot would say, with great rapidity, 'Pieces of eight! pieces of eight! pieces of eight!' till you wondered that it was not out of breath, or till John threw his handkerchief over the cage.

Cocky Bennet in his last years.

'Now, that bird,' he would say, 'is, maybe, 200 years old, Hawkins — they lives for ever mostly; and if anybody's seen more wickedness, it must be the devil himself. She's sailed with England, the great Cap'n England, the pirate. She's been at Madagascar, and at Malabar, and Surinam, and Providence, and Portobello.'

Parrots have been well-established pets for centuries. The Greeks first encountered them after Alexander the Great reached India, and the king is credited with giving them as gifts. His army brought them back to Europe, and the Alexandrine parakeet is still named in his honour. Aristotle notes that 'in general all the crook-taloned birds are short-necked and flat-tongued and given to mimicry. For such too is the Indian bird, the parrot, that is said to be human-tongued, and it becomes even more outrageous after drinking wine.' The Romans adored them. The first-century poet Statius wrote a eulogy to his friend Melior's parrot, which begins with these lines:

Parrot, parrot, king of birds, fluent favourite of your master; parrot, skilled to mimic the accents of man, what power by too swift a fate has stilled your voice? Poor thing, only yesterday, though doomed to die, you had a place at our feast. Beyond the midnight we saw you ranging the couches and tasting the good cheer. Greetings, too, and well-conned words you repeated. To-day the dateless silence of death seals all that melody.

However, Pliny relates that the Romans could use harsh techniques to get their birds to speak:

There are some birds that can imitate the human voice; the parrot, for instance, which can even engage in conversation. India sends us this bird, which is called by the name of 'sittaces'. The body is green all over, only it is marked with a ring of red around the neck. It will duly salute an emperor, and pronounce the words it has heard spoken; it is rendered especially frolicsome under the influence of wine. Its head is as hard as its beak and this, when it is being taught to talk, is beaten with a rod of iron for it feels no other blows.

A parrot adorns a capital 'N' in this thirteenth-century English manuscript of works by Aristotle and others. (*Courtesy of the British Library illuminated manuscripts collection www.bl.uk*)

Yet second-century Roman writer Apuleius warns that teaching parrots bad language, though entertaining initially, can prove annoying:

> Teach a parrot to curse and it will curse continually, making night and day hideous with its imprecations. Cursing becomes its natural note and its ideal of melody. When it has repeated all its curses, it repeats the same strain again. Should you desire to rid yourself of its bad language, you must either cut out its tongue or send it back as soon as possible to its native woods.

Top talker

Britain's most talkative parrot was an African grey named Prudle, who entered the *Guinness Book of World Records* for having the widest spoken vocabulary of any bird at about 800 words. More recently, a New York parrot of the same species called N'kisi is said to use 950 words.

One of the earliest mentions of the parrot in the UK is in the lengthy satirical poem *Speke Parrot* by Henry VIII's poet laureate, John Skelton. This seems to have been composed in around the 1510s, so parrots must have been familiar enough in England by this date. An example verse, in slightly modernised form, describes a Tudor parrot's cage and its interaction with people:

> *A cage curiously carved, with silver, pine,*
> *Properly painted, to be my coverture;*
> *A mirror of glass, that I may look therein;*
> *These maidens fill gently with many a diverse flower*
> *Freshly they dress and make sweet my bower,*
> *With, 'Speke, Parrot, I pray you,' full courteously they say;*
> *'Parrot is a goodly bird, a pretty popinjay.'*

Henry VIII himself owned an African grey parrot, and James V of Scotland had similar pets at around the same time because royal accounts show payment to Thomas Kellis, keeper of the king's parakeets. An amusing tale about Henry VIII's bird was related by the sixteenth-century German naturalist Conrad Gesner. Here it is retold in English by British ornithologist Francis Willughby:

> I shall not think much to set down one very pleasant story, which Gesner saith was told him by a certain friend, of a parrot which fell out of King Henry VIII's Palace at Westminster into the River of Thames that runs by, and then very seasonably remembring the words it had often heard some, whether in danger or in jest, use, cried out amain: 'A boat, a boat, for twenty pound!' A certain experienced boatman made thither presently, took up the bird, and restored it to the king, to whom he knew it belonged, hoping for as great a reward as the bird had promised. The king

African grey parrot.

agreed with the boatman that he should have as the bird being asked anew should say. And the bird answers: 'Give the knave a groat'.

The age of discovery in Europe began to excite renewed interest in exotic birds, as explorers investigated new areas of the globe and brought back colourful avian fauna. They became rare and expensive symbols of wealth and status. The enthusiasm for these pet birds grew and reached its height in the nineteenth and early twentieth centuries, leading to the development of a whole industry to supply parrots, together with suitable cages and specially formulated food. Queen Victoria and many of her family owned parrots, including her mother and her son, Prince Alfred. According to her diaries, Victoria owned at least four: a Brazilian blue-headed parrot named Pedro; a pink and grey parrot (which was probably a galah); a scarlet macaw; and finally 'a most delightful lory which is so tame that it remains on your hand'.

An entry from Victoria's diary in 1838 is one of many in which the queen introduces her beloved birds to intimates of the royal household, in this case the Prime Minister, Lord Melbourne:

We talked also of my parrots; he likes my pink and grey one so much etc. After dinner I had my large macaw brought in, on his stand, who Lord M. had never

PARROT

Feed on Capern's Parrot Food
In Packets only

Parrots were popular pets in Edwardian times, as this postcard and advert for parrot food demonstrates.

Queen Victoria owned a scarlet macaw.

seen; he was perfectly quiet. 'A magnificent bird; beautiful fellow,' Lord M. said, in looking at him; he certainly is, his plumage is so brilliant; he is not an ill-natured bird, and allowed Major Keppell to stroke him. 'You should show confidence in them,' said Lord M., 'and conquer them by their vanity, by praising their beauty; they can't bear derision.'

Parrots have proved popular pets with American presidents as well. John F. Kennedy owned two parakeets – Bluebell and Marybelle – and Eisenhower had one named Gabby. Presidents McKinley, Grant and Madison, amongst others, also owned parrots. Yet perhaps the most famous presidential bird was Poll, a parrot owned by Andrew Jackson. The seventh president of the USA had been a soldier and had no doubt become accustomed to using some fairly colourful vocabulary in the field, which his parrot duly copied. Poll was present at Jackson's funeral and, to the horror of those assembled, chose this solemn occasion to suddenly let loose a stream of foul language. A minister who was present recalled the event:

Before the sermon and while the crowd was gathering, a wicked parrot that was a household pet, got excited and commenced swearing so loud and long as to disturb the people, and had to be carried from the house.

Wild parrots of the UK

Unlike our ancestors, you no longer need to venture to exotic climates in order to see flocks of parrots flying in the wild. The ring-necked parakeet has been breeding in the UK since about 1970 and now numbers many thousands. Although the bulk of the population lives in Kent, Surrey, Sussex and the London suburbs, they have been seen far further afield. The bird comes originally from Africa and the Indian subcontinent, but the UK population seems to have grown from a small nucleus of escaped caged birds.

*D*espite its origins thousands of miles away on the Indian subcontinent, the peacock was known to the Anglo-Saxons, who called it the *po* or *pauo*, a word derived from the bird's Roman name, *pavo*. Technically, the word 'peacock' describes the male of the species only, the female being the 'peahen', and together they are termed 'peafowl'. However, in modern popular usage the word 'peacock' is often taken to encompass both sexes. Only the male has the resplendent tail for which this bird is so famous and it is not surprising that such a beautiful creature has become the national bird of India.

The peacock was familiar to the ancient Greeks, but the Romans particularly seemed to favour the bird. One of the most famous tales about the peacock comes from the

Roman mosaic with peacock at Sabratha, Libya.

Greco-Roman world. Zeus, the king of the gods, was in love with a nymph named Io but he turned her into a cow to hide her from his wife, Hera. The queen knew what was going on, and was not fooled, so she ordered a remarkable being named Argus to guard the animal. Argus had 100 eyes and could keep watch around the clock. In order to rescue his lover, Zeus instructed the god Hermes to lull Argus to sleep with music and then kill him. When Hera returned, she was so upset by the death of the loyal Argus that she transformed his eyes into the beautiful jewels of the peacock's tail so that no one would forget his faithfulness.

The peacock has been a symbol of wealth, beauty and power across a surprisingly wide geography. At least one Viking warrior is known to have been buried with a peacock: the bird's bones were unearthed in a ship burial dated to about AD 900 at Gokstad in Norway. Peacock feathers have long been used as adornments for hats and jewellery, and medieval knights even decorated their helmets with them. The Mughal emperors of Delhi had a peacock throne studded with jewels, which was later stolen by the Persians, and 'Mad' King Ludwig of Bavaria also had a peacock throne at Linderhof Castle. The bird has adorned the currencies of many nations – ancient Rome, India, Sri Lanka, Macedonia, Myanmar, and even Eire.

Peacocks were difficult and costly to obtain in medieval England, so a consummate display of flamboyance was to go to the expense of obtaining these beautiful birds simply to eat them. The receipts for the coronation of Richard III in 1483, for example, reveal that forty-eight peacocks were bought for the royal banquet. The cooked birds were decorated with their handsome feathers to create a magnificent spectacle for the diners. Peacocks were still being eaten by British monarchs as late as the reign of George III.

In former times, there were some odd beliefs about the flesh of the peacock – in particular, that it never decayed. St Augustine of Hippo wrote in the fifth century:

> For who but God the Creator of all things has given to the flesh of the peacock its antiseptic property? This property, when I first heard of it, seemed to me incredible; but it happened at Carthage that a bird of this kind was cooked and served up to me, and, taking a suitable slice of flesh from its breast, I ordered it to be kept, and when it had been kept as many days as make any other flesh stinking, it was produced and set before me, and emitted no offensive smell. And after it had been laid by for thirty days and more, it was still in the same state; and a year after, the same still, except that it was a little more shrivelled, and drier.

This curious tale led to the peacock becoming symbolic of immortality and it appears in Renaissance paintings to symbolise resurrection and eternal life. Another odd belief concerned the peacock's feet – a story that was used by Christians to provide moral instruction about pride and humility. In the thirteenth century, the monk Bartholomew Anglicus described how the peacock disliked its own ugly feet, which contrasted so sharply with its beautiful feathers that they greatly upset the bird:

The peacock hath an unsteadfast and evil-shapen head, as it were the head of a serpent, and with a crest. And he hath a simple pace, and small neck, raised up, and a blue breast, and a tail full of beauty, distinguished on high with wonderful fairness. And he hath foulest feet and wrinkled. And he wondereth of the fairness of his feathers, and raises them up, as it were in a circle about his head, and then he looketh to his feet, and seeth the foulness of his feet, and like as he were ashamed, he letteth his feathers fall suddenly: and all the tail downward, as though he took no heed of the fairness of his feathers. And he hath an horrible voice. As one sayeth: he hath a voice of a fiend, head of a serpent, pace of a thief.

An eighteenth-century version of Bartholomew's concluding adage observes that the peacock had the plumage of an angel, the voice of a demon, and the stomach of a thief. On the latter point, peacocks certainly seem to have a habit of eating almost anything thrown to them.

Mayura Rashka mask.

The peacock has other religious connections outside Christianity. On the Indian subcontinent, many Hindu gods have links with the peacock: Krishna often sports a peacock feather in his headband, and the war god Kartikeya even rides a peacock. In Sri Lanka, the peacock demon, Mayura Raksha, brings peace and prosperity. In Tibetan Buddhism the peacock is believed to be able to ingest poison and transmute it into beauty, which has become an allegory for wisdom: dealing with life's difficulties in order to follow the Buddhist path. In the Jewish *Torah*, the wealth of King Solomon is illustrated by the fact that he could import 'gold and silver, ivory and monkeys, and peacocks'.

Art Nouveau era cover of a French magazine with peacock (1903).

Portrayals of the peacock for artistic purposes have long been popular. The bird often appears in Roman mosaics and paintings, for example, where its eye-catching beauty helped to enliven a floor or wall in the house of the wealthy. However, Renaissance and Baroque painters frequently included the bird in their compositions because of its symbolic association with immortality. Hence, Biblical scenes or depictions of saints often include a peacock lurking somewhere in the picture. From the eighteenth century onwards, the peacock might be included in general studies of birds or in portraits to illustrate the wealth of the sitter since they were commonly kept in menageries or as garden ornaments. By the late nineteenth and early twentieth centuries, the peacock had become a popular motif for the Aesthetic Movement, and James McNeill Whistler's *Peacock Room*, painted in Kensington in 1876–77, is one of the most famous surviving Aesthetic interiors. The peacock captured perfectly the elegant and stylish ethos of Art Nouveau and seemed to become the movement's unofficial emblem, as it was constantly represented in items as diverse as magazine and book covers, jewellery, clothing, table lamps, ceramics, and advertising posters amongst much else.

The beauty of the peacock has led to it becoming a synonym for vanity, pride or ostentation. We talk of someone 'strutting like a peacock'. Images dating back to at least the sixteenth century commonly show the deadly sin of pride as a woman wearing peacock plumes or standing next to a peacock. In the seventeenth century, there was a proverb: 'Men who make peacocks of their wives make woodcocks of themselves.' The woodcock is a remarkably dull bird in comparison with the peacock.

One of the more notable people in recent history to make use of the bird was Elvis Presley, who famously wore a white jumpsuit emblazoned with a blue and gold peacock design during his 1974 tours. It cost him $10,000, the most he ever paid for an item of clothing. He also kept live peacocks in the grounds of his home, Gracelands, and the living room there features a huge stained-glass doorway with a peacock design. For Elvis, the peacock represented, perhaps, flamboyance, fun, and a sense of achievement. In more modern times, the peacock has often been used in advertising to convey luxury or privilege.

The peacock has been widely used in advertising from the nineteenth to the twenty-first centuries to indicate luxury or 'the best'. This advert is from 1889.

Peregrine

*T*his bird's name is taken from the Latin *peregrinus*, meaning 'from strange parts'. The scholar John Selden explained in 1612, 'the reason of the name of peregrin's is given, for that they come from remote and unknowne places.' These large falcons nest in inaccessible locations such as steep cliffs, and they hunt over a large territory; in addition, people noticed that outside the breeding season individual falcons could wander enormous distances. Hence, the word 'peregrine' was also used to describe pilgrims or those travelling great distances to a new area. Chaucer mentions the bird in his *Canterbury Tales*, where a 'faukon peregryn' is described as 'of fremde land' (from a foreign land).

A peregrine owned by Henry IV of France provides a notable example of the great distances that the bird can cover. This falcon bore a leg ring identifying her royal owner when she escaped from the king's palace at Fontainebleau, south of Paris, in 1595. Remarkably, this peregrine turned up the next day on the island of Malta, 1,350 miles away.

It is easy to admire the power, beauty and flying agility of the peregrine. In ancient Egypt, the people worshipped a god, Horus, who is usually depicted with the head of a falcon. It is not entirely certain which bird inspired this depiction, but in many portrayals the head is very similar to that of a peregrine. Appropriately enough, given the falcon connection, Horus was the god of the sky, of hunting, and of war.

Peregrines were especially prized in falconry, a pursuit that was devised in the east probably in the second millennium before Christ. It may have been conceived originally in Mesopotamia or Mongolia. When Marco Polo visited Kublai Khan in the thirteenth century, falconry was already firmly established there. He recorded that if the Mongol emperor went hunting he was 'attended by full 10,000 falconers, who carry with them a vast number of gyrfalcons, peregrine falcons and saker falcons, as well as vultures, in order to pursue the game along the banks of the river.'

Falconry is first mentioned in England during the reign of eighth-century king Ethelbert II of Kent. Peregrine bones have also been found in Viking settlements in Shetland dating from the ninth and tenth centuries, although the significance of this is uncertain. Anglo-Saxon manuscripts from

Horus, the falcon-headed god of ancient Egypt.

the tenth century illustrate English nobles hunting with birds of prey, and the Bayeux Tapestry notably shows King Harold riding with a falcon. After the Norman Conquest, falconry rose to new heights and was popular throughout the medieval period, and there are many depictions of it as a pastime for royalty and the wealthy landed classes. For example, it is reported of Edward III that:

> The king had thirty falconers on horseback with hawkes, and nine-couple of hounds and as many greyhoundes; so that near every day either he hunted or hawked at the river, as it pleased him. And diverse other of the great lords had hounds and hawks, as well as the king.

Falconers were important men in the king's retinue. The birds themselves were typically used to hunt as entertainment, and the heron was an especially sought foe – it was a large bird that was reckoned to put up a good fight. But falcons could also be used to bring down birds for food such as quails, pigeons or ducks. Many other monarchs particularly enjoyed hawking – and its popularity even extended into the Tudor and Stuart periods: Elizabeth I and James I were notable devotees.

King Stephen of England (1135–54) on his throne with a falcon. (*Courtesy of the British Library illuminated manuscripts collection www.bl.uk*)

Peregrines were not bred in captivity; hence, wild birds were the source for falconry, and certain places in the UK such as north Wales and Scotland were prime sites for capturing them. Generally, young birds were taken before they fledged so they could be trained at an early age. One Victorian writer describes an age-old technique for stealing young birds form the peregrine's usually inaccessible nest:

> A person having reached the top of the rock immediately above the nest, ties a rough blue bonnet, or some similar substance, to a bundle of heather the size of a man's head; then dropping this attached to a rope upon the nest, the young falcons, instead of being frightened, immediately attack it, and, sticking their talons into the cap, hold on courageously and determinedly till they are dragged up to the top of the cliff. Even then it is sometimes necessary to cut the cap to pieces before they will relinquish their hold. In this way the young birds are captured, without risk to the capturer or injury to themselves.

A wild peregrine was sometimes known as a duck hawk or haggard hawk, whilst falconers' terms for young birds included eyass and red falcon. There was a convention that the term 'falcon' applied only to the larger female peregrine, whereas the male bird was known as a tercel. This term is believed to have arisen because male peregrines are about a third smaller than the female, and the Norman French for a third was *terce*. The phrase tercel-gentle was also used to describe the male; 'gentle' meaning noble, to reflect the peregrine's esteemed status. Captive birds were quickly taught to obey their master's commands. All of this explains Juliet's words about Romeo in Shakespeare's famous play; eager to speak to her young man again, she exclaims: 'O, for a falconer's voice, To lure this tassel-gentle back again!' The language of falconry would have been well known to Shakespeare's audience and he uses it often.

A hierarchy of falconry was promulgated, and several different interpretations of it exist. An edited version of one fifteenth-century example is:

> An eagle, vulture or gyrfalcon for an emperor,
> A gyrfalcon tercel for a king,
> A peregrine falcon for a prince,
> A rock falcon tercel for a duke,
> A peregrine tercel for an earl,
> A saker falcon for a knight,
> A lanner falcon for a squire,
> A merlin for a lady,
> A goshawk for a yeoman,
> A sparrowhawk for a priest,
> A musket for a holy water clerk,
> A kestrel for a knave.

A modern falconer with a peregrine.

These hierarchies were not used in practice, and were probably written for amusement. In reality, falconers selected the species that was most appropriate to the quarry and the flying conditions on the day, and the wealthy could afford to buy whichever birds they wanted. However, this, and other evidence, suggests that many levels of society enjoyed falconry apart from the royal entourage, including women and persons of modest means.

Given the importance of falconry in centuries past, it is no surprise that many families' coats of arms include a falcon. Anne Boleyn's heraldic badge, for example, was an upright falcon clutching a royal sceptre.

Despite centuries of royal protection, peregrine numbers began to fall once falconry lost its popularity. They suffered from indiscriminate slaughter by farmers and gamekeepers, the Victorians were keen to own a stuffed one, their eggs were stolen in large numbers by collectors, and the birds were hated by pigeon fanciers. Peregrines, and many other large birds of prey, also suffered a great deal from the indiscriminate use of pesticides in the 1950s, '60s and '70s. Smaller animals ingested modest amounts of pesticide, but as predators at the top of the food chain, peregrines ate large numbers of these creatures so that pesticides accumulated to toxic levels in their bodies. Nowadays, the peregrine population has recovered considerably and inner-city nesting on tall buildings such as churches is well known, where these falcons are often welcomed as a natural method to cull urban pigeons.

Pheasant

*T*his bird's name is believed to be derived from a community on the river Phasis in the kingdom of Colchis (modern Georgia), where the bird was first encountered by ancient Greek settlers who called its *phasianos*. It is not native to Europe, but came originally from Asia. The Greeks and Romans both bred the bird for eating. The Romans seem to have brought a few specimens to the UK, but a bigger population of pheasants was not established until at least the eleventh century. In this period, monastic records from the east of England show that greater numbers of pheasants existed, but were still confined to captivity.

By the twelfth century, the pheasant had become an established luxury food item for the privileged. For example, Richard the Lionheart's foster brother, Alexander Neckham, wrote that the pheasant was a delightful honour to the table and a pleasurable glory to the palate. It is also recorded that on the day of his murder in 1170, Archbishop of Canterbury Thomas Becket dined on pheasant. Most birds seem to have been bred in captivity for many centuries to come. Henry VIII, for instance, employed his own pheasant breeder to ensure the royal tables should be well stocked. More pheasants were gradually brought to the UK and eventually, of course, some escaped the oven and the hunter and established themselves in the wild.

Pheasant hunting has long been popular. In the seventeenth century, the ornithologist Francis Willughby describes one method of capturing them:

Pheasants, partridges, quails, and some other birds, are taken in great numbers with a net they call commonly expegatorium, by the help of a setting-dog, trained up for this sport, who finds out the birds, and when he sees them, either stands still, or lies down on his belly, not going very near them, lest he should spring them; but

The 'Lovell Lectionary' was created around 1200 in southern England and depicts a pheasant and a peacock, showing that both birds were familiar. (*Courtesy of the British Library illuminated manuscripts collection www.bl.uk*)

looking back on the fowler, his master, wags his tail, by which the fowler knows that the birds are near the dog; and so he and his companion run with the net, and cover both birds and dog.

In later centuries, of course, pheasant shooting would become popular and whole industries arose to breed and release these birds simply for wealthy persons to kill them. The flesh of the pheasant has always been prized – this being the original reason for breeding them – but at some pheasant shoots the birds were often shot in vast numbers as entertainment, particularly in the twentieth century, and they could not all be eaten. One shooting party attended by George V in 1913 reputedly killed nearly 4,000 pheasants in one day.

Pheasants were reared in very large numbers to supply the needs of the shooters, and inevitably the gamekeepers appointed to patrol these estates came into conflict with others who saw the pheasant as food rather than sport. Firstly, the keepers targeted all birds and animals that might take pheasants, so huge numbers of birds of prey, foxes, and other wildlife were slaughtered indiscriminately. Secondly, the gamekeepers had to tackle local people who stole pheasants to eat or sell. The practice of poaching is an old crime, and it has always been punished severely. A law from the reign of Henry VII stated that none were to take pheasants or partridges 'with engines in another man's ground' on pain of a hefty fine. The term 'engines' meant any weapon, trap, net or device used to seize game. Under James I, killing a pheasant attracted a fine of twenty shillings per bird, plus a one-month prison sentence if it was during the pheasant breeding season.

Shooting birds became a popular pastime in the nineteenth century.

The pheasant was considered by most eighteenth- and nineteenth-century writers as a foolish bird because it was easily caught. In 1802, the naturalist George Montagu gave an interesting description of the techniques typically used by poachers over two centuries ago:

> The poacher will catch them in nooses made of wire, horse-hair twisted, and even with a briar set in the like manner at the verge of a wood, for they always run to feed in the adjacent fields morning and evening. Besides this, they are taken by a wire fastened to a long pole, and by that means taken off their roost at night; or, by fixing a bunch of matches lighted at the end of a pole, are suffocated and drop off the perch.

Pigeon

Woodpigeon.

*T*here are a number of species of pigeon and dove found in the UK. Perhaps most familiar are the woodpigeon, the collared dove, and the many varieties of feral pigeon that congregate as flocks in parks and open spaces in cities. Interestingly, the two names given to members of this family of birds have acquired different connotations. The word 'dove' is more commonly used for the positive symbolism associated with them – peace, holiness, beauty – whilst 'pigeon' can be associated with less desirable attributes – nuisance, uncleanliness, greed. The two words have different origins: dove is derived from Anglo-Saxon, and pigeon was probably introduced into English from Norman French after 1066.

The name 'woodpigeon' became generally accepted only in the twentieth century; before this time the bird was known by a whole array of other names. The term in most general use was the ring dove because of the circlet of white feathers around its neck. Other regional names included clatter dove on account of its noisy take-off, timmer doo or cushat (imitative of its call), and culver (an alternative Anglo-Saxon name). The soft musical notes of the many varieties of dove or pigeon are referred to as a 'coo', but it has long been held to have a plaintive quality. Indeed, many old regional names for the woodpigeon, such as quest or queece, are believed to be derived from the Latin *questus* ('lamenting'). The eighteenth-century naturalist Gilbert White described the sound rather poetically: 'Doves coo in an amorous and mournful manner, and are emblems of despairing lovers.'

Those who encourage birds into their gardens may regard the woodpigeon as something of an annoyance because it can quickly gobble up a high proportion of the food left on bird tables. It is also liable to destroy many types of home-grown fruit and vegetables. In fact, the bird has long been regarded as a pest by farmers as it will eat large quantities of many crops including grain, peas, turnips, broccoli, and several varieties of fruit. Gilbert White related a rather unusual tale of the consequences of crop-feasting for one particular woodpigeon:

> One of my neighbours shot a ring dove on an evening as it was returning from feed and going to roost. When his wife had picked and drawn it, she found its craw stuffed with the most nice and tender tops of turnips. These she washed and boiled, and so sat down to a choice and delicate plate of greens, culled and provided in this extraordinary manner.

Woodpigeons were commonly eaten in the past, but diners noticed that what the pigeons ate influenced the taste of their flesh. Many disliked the unusual flavour imparted by a diet of turnips, for example, although Gilbert White admitted that he rather liked it.

Modern history

In 2015, Indian police arrested a pigeon as a suspected spy from Pakistan; they detained the bird although later reported that nothing remarkable was found after it was examined. The following year they brought a second bird into custody that was apparently carrying a note from a militant group threatening the life of India's prime minister, Narendra Modi.

Woodpigeons have been resident in Britain for thousands of years yet the equally familiar collared dove is a newcomer. Although a very common breeding bird in British towns and gardens these days, it only nested in this country for the first time in 1955. The collared dove is slimmer and smaller than the woodpigeon, and is named because of its little half-circlet of black neck feathers. It came originally from India but began to spread westwards a few centuries ago, reaching the Balkans by the late 1800s. From there it rapidly colonised the rest of Europe in the twentieth century.

Collared dove.

The scientific name for the collared dove is *Streptopelia decaocto*, which has an interesting derivation. The Greek word *streptos* means 'twisted chain' (or collar) and *peleia is* 'dove', but the second part of the name comes from Latin: *deca* means 'ten' and *octo* is 'eight'. Ten and eight, or eighteen. What is the significance of this number? The naturalist that bestowed the collared dove's scientific name liked a myth he had heard about a hardworking servant girl who complained to the gods that she was only paid eighteen pieces of silver a year by her employer. In reply the gods sent out a dove to proclaim the girl's misfortune to the world: *deca octo* is supposed to resemble the collared dove's call.

The feral pigeons that now occur in flocks in many human settlements are often labelled as pests because they can be very numerous and their excrement is damaging and unsightly. They are mostly descended from specially bred domestic varieties of differing colours and appearances that have escaped captivity. In the past, the selective breeding of pigeons to produce attractive plumage was a very popular pastime. 'Pigeon fanciers' created a great diversity of appearance. There were pure white doves and a wide range of other colours; fan-tailed varieties were popular; breeds such as the turbit had crests and frills of feathers; other forms had coloured eye rings; perhaps most bizarrely, the pouter pigeons inflate their necks so that they look as if they have an enormous chest and head. Over time, people forgot the natural source of these breeding birds that have now produced so many different varieties. However, they are all ultimately derived from a species that is not so frequently seen in the wild in the UK because it is confined

Feral pigeons are a well-established feature of some tourist attractions such as Trafalgar Square in London.

to high sea cliffs – the rock dove. This bird has been common on the shores of the Mediterranean for thousands of years and their breeding in captivity may have begun in ancient Egypt. Indeed, the pigeon lays claim to being the oldest bird domesticated by humans.

Pigeon fanciers meet at an evening bird show in 1822 (top). Various breeds of the pouter pigeon can inflate their crops to enlarge their necks (below).

Pigeons are not just bred for their appearance: birds are also used for racing. One variety in particular, the racing homer, is valued for its speed, endurance, and strong homing instincts. From the nineteenth century onwards, pigeon racing became a recognised and popular pastime, with the fastest birds becoming much-prized avian celebrities. The advent of the train was important to the sport's success because it meant that pigeons could quickly be taken a long distance from the finishing post for release en masse.

The dove and Noah's Ark. This stained glass window is in St Leonard's Church, Bursledon.

Dove and Christianity

The dove is the bird most commonly shown in stained glass windows in Christian churches, because it is associated with reconciliation and peace. In the Old Testament, Noah released a dove from the ark and it came back with an olive leaf, indicating not only that the waters of the flood were receding but that God had forgiven humankind so that people were once again allowed to settle upon the land.

   The dove also represents the Holy Spirit – one element of the Christian Trinity together with God the Father and his son, Jesus. In a well-known passage from St Matthew's Gospel, Jesus is baptised in the river Jordan by John the Baptist:

   And Jesus when he was baptised, went up straightaway out of the water: and lo, the heavens were opened unto him, and he saw the Spirit of God descending like a dove, and lighting upon him: And lo, a voice from heaven, saying 'This is my beloved Son, in whom I am well pleased.'

Both of these Biblical stories are commonly depicted in church windows. The dove was also held to represent the human soul. Because of all these sacred connections, no witch or demon was said to be able to assume the form of a dove.

Perhaps the most important role that these birds played in former times was also a function of their ability to return unerringly to their homes. These homing pigeons or 'carrier pigeons' were the basis of one of the oldest forms of long-distance communication between people, which seems perhaps to have originated in the Middle East or North Africa.

Lancastrian organ maker Thomas Dallam travelled to Constantinople on a mission for Elizabeth I in the late sixteenth century and he marvelled that the Turks seemed to have a mysterious method of sending messages long distances at great speed:

The first of June there was letters conveyed very strangely from Aleppo to Iskendurun, the which is three score and twelve miles distance. After I had been there a little while, I perceived that it was an ordinary thing. For, as we were sitting in our merchant's house talking, and pigeons were a-feeding in the house before us, there came a white cote pigeon flying in and light on the ground amongst his fellows, the which, when one of the merchants saw, he said: 'Welcome, Honest Tom,' and taking him up, there was tied with a thread under his wing a letter, the bigness of a twelve pence, and it was dated but four hours before. After that I saw the like done, and always in four hours.

Some birds travelled remarkably long distances on their missions. A pigeon released by polar explorer Sir John Ross from the Canadian Arctic Circle in 1850 returned to its dovecote in Ayrshire in around seven days. It had maybe secured a lift on a passing ship for part of the way, but the pigeon had journeyed about 2,500 miles across the Atlantic, although unfortunately it had lost the messages it was carrying.

Pigeons came into their own as messengers in the First World War. Radio was unreliable and both the Allies and the Germans made use of pigeons to carry vital messages. The British even adapted London buses to serve as mobile pigeon lofts. When the Second World War loomed, the military were keen to establish an organised approach to managing the birds and created the National Pigeon Service to ensure that sufficient trained birds were available. The service utilised around a quarter of a million birds during the conflict, and it was taken up by the army, navy and air force. Some of the pigeons performed quite heroic exploits. Mary, a bird owned by shoemaker Charlie Brewer from Exeter, was wounded in action three times. She was hit by gunshot and had part of a wing blown off, was attacked by a hawk, and had shrapnel fragments removed from her body. She also survived having her pigeon loft bombed by the Luftwaffe. Despite all this suffering, she made it through the war and was even decorated. Mary and thirty-one other carrier pigeons from the Second World War were awarded the Dickin Medal for conspicuous gallantry or devotion to duty by the People's Dispensary for Sick Animals.

Curious roles for a bird

Pigeons are readily available and easy to train and so have been enlisted for a variety of more unusual purposes, none stranger perhaps than the guided rockets devised for the US military in the Second World War. In so-called 'Project Pigeon', each missile had a cockpit that accommodated birds trained to recognise a live projected image of the target. They would peck at the picture to keep it central and this would maintain the projectile's course to its final destination. It was a suicide mission for the unfortunate pigeons, of course, and although testing showed that the mechanism worked, the military hierarchy remained sceptical and it was never used in anger.

At the beginning of the twentieth century, a German inventor patented the use of a lightweight miniature camera that was strapped to pigeons. It had an automatic timing mechanism so that the birds could take aerial photographs. Pigeons have also carried medicines to the needy, been trained to perform in circuses or as part of magicians' acts, and the superior vision of these birds even led to their being strapped under helicopters by the US Coast Guard in the late 1970s to help search for people lost at sea.

Carrier pigeons being taken to the front line in about 1915. (*Courtesy of Library of Congress, Washington*)

Robin

Statue of Robin Hood in Nottingham.

*I*n the UK, where many birds are apt to have rather dull plumage, the robin's splendid orange-red breast is an appealing splash of colour that is frequently seen in gardens, parks, and the countryside. Another attractive feature is that the robin seems to have a quite distinct personality. Its beautiful song is often described as one of the most joyful of British birds, and robins will often come quite close to people, which makes them seem friendly and trusting. Yet despite an apparently cheery disposition, robins are feisty and, though small, they defend their territories quite assertively. With these characteristics, it is no wonder that although the UK has no 'official' national bird, public votes in 1960 and 2015 nominated the robin as the nation's favourite: a bright little bird that knows how to stand up for itself.

The popularity of robins dates back hundreds of years and, unlike many other birds, they have rarely been persecuted in the UK. Indeed, to harm the robin was considered unlucky, with various grim outcomes forecast for the persecutor. With good reason, the poet William Blake wrote the lines:

> *A robin redbreast in a cage*
> *Puts all Heaven in a rage.*

But the robin has not always been known by its now very familiar name. In Anglo-Saxon times the bird was called the *rudduc*, meaning something like 'little red one', and the old regional names of ruddock or reddock attest to the persistence of this influence until quite recently. By the sixteenth century, terms such as 'Robin Ruddock' and 'Robin Redbreast' were in use as friendly pet names, with the latter becoming gradually dominant. Robin was an affectionate diminutive for men called Robert, gaining popularity from figures such as the cheeky Robin Goodfellow ('Puck') or the charismatic people's hero Robin Hood. The robin acquired similar pet names in other European countries: 'Peter Ronsmad' in Norway, for example, and 'Thomas Gierdet' in Germany.

This trend towards adopting human nicknames for birds of character has, in this country, given rise to other enduring examples such as Jenny Wren. In the case of Robin Redbreast, it was in fact the term 'redbreast' that initially tended to predominate as the formal title for the bird. Natural history books generally identify the bird as 'redbreast' until the end of the nineteenth century. Before the twentieth century, the term 'robin' was a more informal name, used for example in popular verses such as this one:

> *The north wind doth blow,*
> *And we shall have snow,*
> *And what will the robin do then,*
> *Poor thing?*

Perhaps the most famous use is in the many stanzas of a well-known nursery rhyme that probably first appeared in the eighteenth century:

Who killed Cock Robin?
I, said the sparrow,
With my bow and arrow,
I killed Cock Robin.

… All the birds of the air
Fell a-sighing and a-sobbing,
When they heard the bell toll
For poor Cock Robin.

In this rather strange story, various birds and other animals volunteer to take care of the funeral arrangements after the sparrow confesses to murdering the robin: the owl offers to dig the grave, the rook to act as parson, the dove will be chief mourner, and the kite agrees to carry the coffin.

English poets were particularly enamoured of the robin, and the bird is often mentioned. Thomas Gray's *Elegy in a Country Churchyard*, for example, includes the delightful lines:

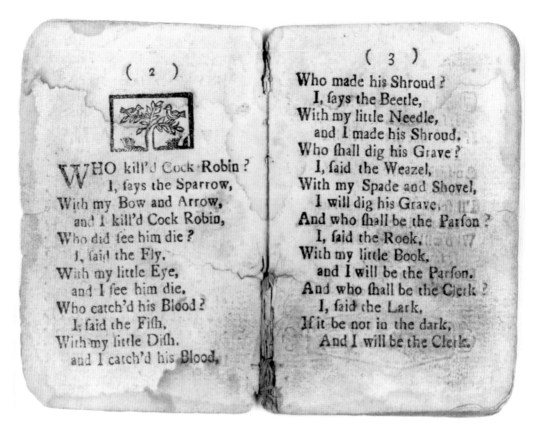

Early edition of *Who Killed Cock Robin?* from 1780. (*Courtesy of Library of Congress, Washington*)

> *There scatter'd oft, the earliest of the year,*
> *By hands unseen are show'rs of violets found;*
> *The redbreast loves to build and warble there,*
> *And little footsteps lightly print the ground.*

Apart from Blake and Gray, many other poets mention the robin – Spenser, Pope, Keats, Cowper, Coleridge; Thomas Hardy wrote a whole poem entitled *The Robin*, although it's not one of his best. However, of all the English poets, Wordsworth is by far the most enthusiastic, and notably includes the bird in fourteen of his poems, including *The Redbreast Chasing the Butterfly*:

> *Art thou the bird whom Man loves best,*
> *The pious bird with the scarlet breast,*
> *Our little English Robin;*
> *The bird that comes about our doors*
> *When autumn winds are sobbing?*

It's hard to know whether it was the popularity of robins that led to the many folklore tales about their good nature, or whether the tales came first and fuelled the high opinion that our ancestors had of the bird. Probably a bit of both. Many stories explain that the robin was originally a rather dull-coloured bird that acquired his red breast by his good deeds. Perhaps the most popular account tells how a robin tried to pull thorns from Christ's head during the crucifixion and was splashed with his blood, or alternatively the bird injured himself on a thorn while singing to Christ on the cross. However, it was also said that the robin was the first to carry the knowledge of fire to humans but burned his chest in the process of carrying a flame. Some variants on this tale suggest that the wren was the fire-bringer and that the robin burned himself while helping. The connection with the wren is quite enduring in folklore. The two birds were said to be of special interest to God, and in one popular old adage were as important to him as chickens were to his people:

> *The robin red-breast and the wren,*
> *Are God Almighty's cock and hen;*
> *The martin and the swallow*
> *Are the next two birds that follow.*

Strangely, robins also had a rather unusual connection with death. If a robin found an unattended human corpse, the story went, he would try to cover it as a mark of respect and kindness to the deceased. In the traditional tale *Babes in the Wood*, which dates to at least the sixteenth century, two abandoned children die in a forest and are buried by robins. Yet there are multiple references to this type of behaviour by other authors so it was obviously a well-established belief. For example, seventeenth-century poet Robert Herrick wrote this verse entitled *To Robin Red-breast*:

> *Laid out for dead, let thy last kindness be*
> *With leaves and moss-work for to cover me,*
> *And while the wood-nymphs my cold corpse inter*
> *Sing thou my dirge, sweet-warbling chorister!*
> *For epitaph, in foliage, next write this:*
> *Here, here the tomb of Robin Herrick is!*

Similarly, Michael Drayton included these two lines in his satirical poem *The Owl*, in 1604:

> *Covering with mosse the dead's unclosed eye:*
> *The little Red-breast teacheth charytie.*

Death of a queen

One robin gained fame in 1695 for singing every day in Westminster Abbey following the interment of Queen Mary II. This bird was dubbed the 'Westminster Wonder', and regularly alighted on the pinnacle of the queen's mausoleum, 'where he is seen and heard to sing, and will not depart the place, to the admiration of many beholders.'

Was this sweet song perhaps a sign of heaven's approval of the drastic measures the queen and the country had taken to oust Catholic James II by force? The exiled king was Mary's father, but she and her husband William III were protestants and James was to be the last Catholic monarch.

The 'Westminster Wonder'. (*Courtesy of Wellcome Library, London*)

More cheerfully, the robin is closely associated with Christmas cards and each year many of them carry the image of this much-loved bird. There are a number of reasons for this. Robins sing all year round, including in the winter, and their bright appearance, cheerful song, and confiding nature are particularly welcome in the dark, cold days of mid-winter when people are often specially roused to feed them. Robins traditionally have a number of Christian connections too, as already described. However, it has been suggested that another reason for the bird's portrayal on Christmas cards is that until the early 1860s, Victorian postmen wore red coats that may have earned them the name of 'robins'. The novelist Anthony Trollope worked for the Post Office, and may have helped to popularise the nickname in his immensely successful book *Framley Parsonage*, published in 1861, in which he describes letter-carriers as 'Robin postman' or 'Robin post-boy':

> But on the next morning there came to him tidings by the hands of Robin postman, which for a long while upset his plans. The letter was from Exeter.

Postmen were particularly active at Christmas, of course, and robins feature on cards from the very earliest occasions on which they were given, around 1860. Another reason that robins may be associated with Christmas is that in Victorian times special meals were sometimes organised by benevolent groups for the impoverished and starving children living on the streets. These often happened during the festive season and were known as 'robin dinners'. Hence the robin came to be linked to good will and charity at Christmas.

The special relationship

Robins often build nests in unusual places. To the delight of William IV, robins built a nest in a shot hole in the mast of HMS *Victory* that he had had transported to his garden. The robin's tameness has led it to go inside people's houses and select intimate and sometimes rather inconvenient places to raise a family. Eighteenth- and nineteenth-century authors often noted robins entering homes when a window or door was left open in spring. Homeowners might suddenly find a nest amongst family books, within the folds of a curtain, on a shelf, inside an old shoe, in a letterbox, or hidden within the branches of a pot plant.

Churches were sometimes chosen for nesting or residence as well. In the early nineteenth century, a pair of robins built a nest next to the bible at Hampton parish church in Warwickshire. The vicar would not allow them to be disturbed and used a different bible until the brood had fled the nest. Parishioners usually felt that the presence of a robin amongst the congregation was a blessing, but one clergyman didn't agree. Dr George Wilkins, Archdeacon of St Mary's, Nottingham, was annoyed by a robin that fluttered around and sang during his sermons, so one Sunday morning in 1835, he had the bird shot. It provoked outrage. One local reporter wrote:

> We know that hundreds of the frequenters of St Mary's have delighted in the cheerful warblings of this very bird; we dare say much more than in the sermons of the Doctor himself – and can any one of these people ever see him again without thinking to himself 'Who killed Cock Robin?' … Small as is the fact of killing a robin, we feel assured that the killing of it in such a place, by a clergyman, on such a day, and in violation of a national and more than national attachment to this bird, will have an influence on the general opinion of the Doctor's disposition that we would not be the object of for all the feathered fowl in the kingdom.

Robins have been popular images on Christmas cards since they were first introduced.

Sparrow

Male house sparrow.

*T*he sparrow has one of the oldest bird names in the English language. Anglo-Saxon texts from as far back as the early eighth century mention the *spearwa* or *spearua*. For example, in Bede's *Ecclesiastical History of the English People*, completed in about 731 CE, he recounts the poetic words of one of the advisers of King Edwin of Northumbria at a conference in 627 CE:

> The present life of man, o king, seems to me, in comparison of that time which is unknown to us, like to the swift flight of a sparrow through the room wherein you sit at supper in winter, with your commanders and ministers, and a good fire in the midst, whilst the storms of rain and snow prevail abroad. The sparrow, I say, flying in at one door, and immediately out at another, whilst he is within, is safe from the wintry storm; but after a short space of fair weather, he immediately vanishes out of your sight, into the dark winter from which he had emerged. So this life of man appears for a short space, but of what went before, or what is to follow, we are utterly ignorant.

In the past, everyone could relate to the sparrow, because it was a common and familiar creature that dwelt around people's homes. Hence it was often used in allegories such as the example quoted by Bede. Another well-known example comes from the Christian Bible, where Christ reassures his disciples that every person is important to God:

> Can you not buy two sparrows for a penny? And yet not one falls to the ground without your Father knowing. Why, every hair on your head has been counted. So there is no need to be afraid; you are worth more than hundreds of sparrows.

Around the world, the sparrow has been used to symbolise everyday problems and everyday people in various sayings or proverbs. Some examples include:

- A spoken word is not a sparrow – once it flies out, you can't catch it. (Russia)
- Two sparrows on the same ear of corn are not long friends. (France)
- The sick sparrow never forgets a kindness. (Japan)
- The old age of an eagle is better than the youth of a sparrow. (Greece)
- Old sparrows are difficult to tame. ('Auld sparrows is ill tae tame'; Scotland)

Sparrows used to be so common in London that cockneys identified themselves with these cheeky, vocal little birds, even using the name as a form of endearment: 'Hello, me old cock sparrow.' The celebrated French singer Edith Piaf was nicknamed 'the little sparrow' reputedly because of her petite stature and her nervous disposition in the early days of her career, but perhaps it was also inspired by her humble origins. The simple, lowly sparrow was even kept as a pet. The Roman poet Catullus wrote about one owned by his lover, Lesbia; and John Skelton, the Poet Laureate in Henry VIII's reign, composed a lengthy eulogy to a pet called Philip Sparrow who was killed by a cat. Here are a few sample lines:

I wept and I wailed,
The tears down, haled;
But nothing it availed
To call Philip again,
Whom Gyb our cat hath slayne.

It is possible that 'Philip' was a generic English sobriquet for the sparrow in centuries past – rather like Robin Redbreast or Jack Daw – because several writers use this name when referring to the bird.

Little Cock Sparrow was a children's song or nursery rhyme that was once very popular, especially in the nineteenth and early twentieth centuries, but it is now rarely heard. It tells the story of a little boy who bravely sets out to hunt a sparrow with his bow and arrow. It may originate from an eighteenth-century play by Samuel Foote, but an early version of the song from 1811 concludes with this verse:

Edwardian illustration for children's rhyme *Little Cock Sparrow*.

Then this little boy cry'd as his bow-string he drew,
This little cock sparrow shall make me a stew,
And his giblets shall make me a little pie too.
But he miss'd his aim, broke his arrow in two!
Cried the little cock sparrow, I'll not make your stew,
For I'll stay no longer, be damned if I do!

The sparrow war

Before the siege of Troy, the ancient Greeks assembled 1,000 ships at the town of Aulis. While they made sacrifices to Zeus to bless their endeavours, an immense snake was seen to climb a nearby tree and eat eight baby sparrows and then the mother of the helpless chicks as well. The warriors had an experienced prophet or 'augur' with them called Calchas, and he knew what the gods meant by this heavenly sign:

> 'Oh Greeks, we shall conquer! Troy is ours, but not without a long delay. The nine birds show that we will have to labour for nine years, but our arms will be crowned with success in the tenth year.'

And, of course, Calchas's interpretation was right.

The serpent eats the sparrows.

The history of birds and humans constantly reveals rather bizarre or unexpected connections. These days, who might have guessed that besides representing the 'everyday person', our ancestors also associated the sparrow with lust? This relationship probably arose because house sparrows live in large collectives, often near houses, where they copulate frequently and reproduce quickly. Thus the sexual activity of sparrows is very obvious, but we now know that sparrows are often promiscuous too – copulating with birds other than their designated mate. The ancient Greeks linked the bird with the goddess of love, Aphrodite, whom the Romans called Venus. Aristotle advised that eating sparrows would improve fertility and sexual appetite:

> The following things increase the natural seed [i.e. fertility], stir up sexual passions, and recover the seed again when it is lost, namely eggs, milk, rice boiled in milk; sparrows' brains, flesh, bones and all … And this is an undeniable aphorism, that whatever any creature is addicted unto, they move or excite the man or woman that eats them to do likewise; and therefore partridges, quails and sparrows etc. being

extremely addicted to sexual gratification, they work the same effect on those men and women that eat them.

This association was well known to later writers such as Chaucer and Shakespeare, who made use of it in their works. Chaucer, for example, describes one male character in *The Canterbury Tales* as 'hot and lecherous as a sparrow'. Even 2,000 years after Aristotle, the eating of these birds was still believed to bring on lusty passions in those who consumed them. One seventeenth-century English doctor described sparrows in these words:

Female house sparrow.

They be of a very hot nature … Their flesh is hard to digest, they stir up Venus, especially the cock sparrows. But being boiled in broth, they are restorative, and good for weak or aged persons.

The bad news for the randy sparrow was that all this sexual activity was believed to explain the bird's very short life expectancy.

Special sparrow nets were used to catch these and other small birds, but not exclusively for human consumption, as early ornithologist Francis Willughby recorded:

This net is to be used late in the evening, or early in the morning, by setting it against the eves of thatched houses, stacks, hovels, barns, stables, dove-coats etc. and being so set knocking and thrusting the cross-staves close against the same, making such a noise as may enforce the birds to fly out of their holes or haunts into the net …

The chief benefit of taking birds in this manner is for the mewing of hawks, or getting into lust and strength sick and weak hawks, because with this engine you may take evening and morning so many birds as you please, and give them warm to your hawk, which is the greatest nourishment that can be: raising a hawk soon, and making her mew fast.

Mewing hawks were those unable to hunt while they moulted, so had to be fed by hand.

Sparrows were not always valued, even as food – and nowhere is this more true than in the US. A curious chapter in the history of our human relationship with birds centres on an organisation called the American Acclimatization Society, which operated in the nineteenth century. The society believed that the flora and fauna of Europe ought to be introduced into the US, and it has been suggested that its most enthusiastic president, Eugene Schieffelin, was particularly inspired to ensure that birds mentioned by Shakespeare should colonise America. Although the society failed in its attempts to establish US breeding populations of birds such as the nightingale, it had much more success with the sparrow. In fact, the programme of introduction was far too successful and the population of 'English sparrows' began to rocket out of control. The birds soon became a great nuisance – there were millions of them.

By the turn of the century, there was sufficient concern about the enormous unwanted population of 'English sparrows' that an official US report in 1912 concluded:

English sparrows are abundant in most of the towns of the United States and in many suburban districts. They are noisy, filthy, and destructive. They drive native birds from villages and homesteads. Though they are occasionally valuable as destroyers of noxious insects, all things considered, they do far more harm than good. Practicable methods of dealing with them include destruction of nests, shooting, trapping, and poisoning. Of these, trapping is unquestionably the best. English sparrows are good to eat, and their use as food is recommended because of their nutritive value and as a means of reducing their numbers.

Not only in the US were sparrows subjected to culling. In the UK, members of so-called 'sparrow clubs' hunted and killed the birds because they were believed to eat valuable seeds and grain. The custom was to produce the sparrows' heads as proof of a kill and earn a small reward from the community. For example, in 1865, the chairman of the Shipley Sparrow Club in Yorkshire announced at their annual meeting 'that 10,807 sparrow and other heads had been sent in during the year, that being about 900 more than last year.' There was a resurgence of these clubs in some areas of the UK during the First World War because of the shortage of food. It's a wonder that any survived.

However, eliminating one species can have unforeseen environmental consequences. Sparrows were once very common in China. In fact, one literal translation of the Chinese game mah-jong is 'chattering sparrow', perhaps because the speedy clacking of the tiles is reminiscent of the squabbling sounds from a colony of these birds. Nonetheless, Chairman Mao Zedong had other ideas about them, and in the 1950s he demanded that sparrows be targeted as one of four national pests, along with rats, mosquitoes and flies. The whole country was mobilised to kill them and hundreds of millions of sparrows were eradicated, but the sparrow played a vital part in eradicating insects, which multiplied as a result, and destroyed crops. This contributed to an extreme shortage of food known as the Great Chinese Famine, which began in 1958 and killed as many as 45 million people.

Tiles from the Chinese game of mah-jong – the 'chattering sparrow'.

A curious trip to the opera

Joseph Addison MP was walking the streets of London one day in 1710, when he came across a man carrying a cage filled with small birds. Addison asked him and his companion what the birds were for:

'Sparrows for the opera,' says his friend, licking his lips.
'What, are they to be roasted?'
'No, no,' says the other, 'they are to enter towards the end of the first act, and fly about the stage.'

Intrigued, he went to see the opera and, sure enough, on came the sparrows. Unfortunately, however, the long-term legacy of allowing sparrows to fly freely around inside an opera house did not seem to have been considered:

There have been so many flights of them let loose in this opera, that it is feared the house will never get rid of them; and that in other plays they may make their entrance in very wrong and improper scenes, so as to be seen flying in a lady's bed-chamber, or perching upon a king's throne; besides the inconveniences which the heads of the audience may sometimes suffer from them.

Starling

Our Anglo-Saxon ancestors called this bird the *staer* or *stærlinc*, and 'stare' continued to be an alternative name for the starling that was widely used for many centuries. In the wild, the starling is noted for incorporating frequently heard sounds into its apparently chaotic whistles, clicks and calls and so it is no surprise that pet birds can be taught particular tunes or can even learn to mimic the human voice. In his *Natural History*, the Roman author Pliny recorded that the future emperor Nero and his step-brother kept a starling:

> At the moment that I am writing this, the young Caesars have a starling and some nightingales that are being taught to talk in Greek and Latin. To this end, they are studying their task the whole day: continually repeating the new words that they have learned, and giving utterance to phrases even of considerable length. Birds are taught to talk in a quiet place, and where no other voice can be heard so as not to interfere with their lesson. A person sits by them and continually repeats the words he wishes them to learn while at the same time he encourages them by giving them food.

In 1661, the diarist Samuel Pepys described a visit to his friend, Mrs Martin, and was surprised to find that she had unexpected company:

> Here I was mightily taken with a starling which she hath, that was the king's, which he kept in his bedchamber, and do whistle and talk the most and best that ever I heard anything in my life.

It may seem rather eccentric behaviour for Charles II to have a tame starling in his bedroom, but keeping trained birds indoors was quite common. Nicholas Cox was an eighteenth-century lifestyle adviser for gentlemen, and in his book *The Gentleman's Recreation* he offers guidance to his readers who might wish to acquire one:

> Of the starling. This bird is generally kept by all sorts of people above any other bird for whistling. ... I look upon the starling to be the best, and never heard better than at The Greyhound in St Mary Axe [London], taught and sold by the ingenious master of that house.

Yet perhaps the most famous owner of a starling was the Austrian composer Mozart. He bought his bird from a pet shop in Vienna because it whistled to him a tune from one of his own piano concertos. Mozart kept the starling until it died three years later in 1787. He staged an elaborate funeral for the bird and even wrote a poetic eulogy, which begins: 'Here rests a dear fool: A starling bird still in his prime.' The first piece of music that Mozart composed after the death of his pet was *Ein Musikalischer Spaß* (*A Musical Joke*), a work that is very out of character: repetitive, clumsy, discordant. Some have suggested that this was Mozart's musical tribute to his avian friend or that it was at least partly inspired by the starling's haphazard calls, tunes and vocalisations.

Starlings have inspired other composers too. The hero in Schubert's song cycle *Die Schöne Müllerin* expresses a desire to send a starling to his distant true love. He sings about teaching the starling to say everything he needs his sweetheart to hear, and with all the passion of his heart.

However, starlings mimic a wide range of other sounds, not just music and the human voice. Individuals frequently impersonate snatches of the songs of other birds such as the blackbird, song thrush and finches, and even farmyard animals. They will also replicate inanimate sounds quite faithfully such as mobile phones, ice cream vans, doorbells, creaky gates, and power tools.

In the nineteenth century, the starling was still a popular tame bird, and the expert on caged birds, Johann Bechstein, notes that it has other attractive qualities as a pet besides its ability to impersonate:

> The starling becomes wonderfully familiar in the house; as docile and cunning as a dog, he is always gay, wakeful, soon knows all the inhabitants of the house, remarks their motions and air, and adapts himself to their humours.

Starling populations in the UK have fluctuated a lot over the past two centuries for reasons that are not entirely clear. In Victorian times, fears were expressed that starlings might die out as their numbers seemed to be dwindling so dramatically. In 1892, even Florence Nightingale commented on the drop in bird numbers in a letter to her friend Edmund Verney, both of whom had lived at Claydon House in Buckinghamshire:

I saw a sensible diminution of birds in my last few weeks at Claydon over and above the extraordinary disappearance of the last two years. Some species have entirely disappeared. One wretched half-starved starling who came to my window to beg is the sole representative remaining of the splendid crown of starlings which used to sit or parade along the top of your church tower.

In the twentieth century, the starling population had rallied, only to enter another period of decline by the end of the century – at least as far as urban populations are concerned. However, in the right places, you can still see the mass gatherings of starlings for which this bird has become famous. It is an amazing spectacle to watch thousands of starlings wheeling in flight in unison, like a shoal of fish. It is not a modern phenomenon and has been known about for centuries. By the fifteenth century, the term 'murmuration' was coined to describe an assemblage of starlings. It is a very apt term as it seems to capture the sound of the starlings' constant chattering to each other when they congregate in large numbers.

Starlings of New York

Eugene Schieffelin was a fanatical devotee of Shakespeare and he decided – for reasons only he could ever explain – that the American public ought to be able to see for themselves each of the sixty or so birds that the Bard mentions in his writings. Shakespeare mentions the starling only once, in *Henry IV, Part 1*, where Hotspur conjures up a plan to annoy the sovereign by giving him a starling trained to repeat the name of the king's enemy:

> I'll have a starling shall be taught to speak
> Nothing but 'Mortimer', and give it him
> To keep his anger still in motion.

Because of this single line in an Elizabethan play, Schieffelin released around 100 starlings into Central Park, New York, in 1890 and 1891. The birds multiplied enormously, and today there are hundreds of millions of starlings in the US. So much so, that they have achieved the status of pest, just like the sparrows that Schieffelin's group also introduced. In 1960, a flock of starlings triggered the worst ever airline crash due to birds: hundreds of them were sucked into a plane's engines shortly after take-off from Logan Airport, Boston, causing it to crash into the sea, killing sixty-two people.

Homesick European emigrants took the starling to other countries too in the nineteenth century. Nations such as South Africa, Australia, New Zealand and many of the Caribbean islands now have resident populations.

Swan

Mute swan.

*A*n often repeated tale about the swan is that it can reputedly break a person's leg or arm with one blow of its powerful wings. It's not clear how this myth came into being, but avian bones are hollow and light, so simply not strong enough to fracture the far more robust bones of a healthy human. It's hard to see how a swan could possibly cause so much damage, short of tripping someone up. Perhaps this story arose as a consequence of the renowned aggression of the swan when protecting its nest and young.

The mute swan is one of the UK's biggest birds, and the male can be intimidating when it rears up in front of you – beak gaping, hissing, and wings flapping. The swans in a village near me regularly hold up the traffic when they decide to cross the road; more often than not, they simply stand defiantly in the middle of it until such time as the mood takes them to move on. No one is willing to try to shoo them away. They

Angry swan chasing away an intruder from Charles Darwin's book *The Expression of the Emotions in Man and Animals*.

will sometimes land on motorways too, and refuse to leave, causing long tailbacks. Rail commuters in the UK will also be familiar with occasional delays caused by a 'swan on the line' – there are a number of media stories every year about birds that stubbornly block the path of a train. There are also plenty of tales on the internet about swans attacking people walking along the riverside, canoeists, dogs, model boats and so on.

The truth of it is that, by and large, whilst an individual swan might occasionally give you a fright, a nasty nip, or knock a toddler over, they rarely pose any real danger. Nevertheless, in our modern world, there is a tendency to associate the swan with a certain forcefulness of character, even aggression. Our ancestors, however, viewed the swan very differently.

Swan feathers

Swan feathers were widely used in the past for various purposes. The large, stiff wing feathers were employed as flights for arrows, to make quills for writing, and were tied together to use as dusters and brushes. Swan feathers were considered better quality than goose, and fetched more than twice the price, costing £3 to £5 per thousand in 1854. Other feathers were used for stuffing pillows and mattresses. Birds were not necessarily killed to support this trade. There was a flourishing business on the shores of the Black Sea in the mid-nineteenth century simply to collect the enormous numbers of feathers shed by the many swans that bred there. The bird's skin with myriad tiny feathers still attached was called 'swan down' and was used as ladies' powder puffs, and as a trim for clothing.

The commonest swan in the UK is the mute swan, so called because it is said to utter no sound. Yet, in ancient times it was believed that the swan could foretell its own death, and when imminent the bird would sing a most beautiful song, almost as a reward for a lifetime of silence. This curious belief is the origin of the idiom 'swan song', used to describe a last great performance by someone who is bowing out. Aristotle described the swan's behaviour in his *History of Animals* (350 BC):

> They are musical, and sing chiefly at the approach of death. At this time, they fly out to sea, and men when sailing past the coast of Libya have fallen in with many of them out at sea singing in mournful strains, and have actually seen some of them dying.

Belief in the swan's great singing ability was such that it was associated with the two greatest musicians of the Greco-Roman world, being dubbed the 'bird of Orpheus' or the 'bird of Apollo'. Even though some writers as far back as Pliny questioned the authenticity of the tale, this curious conviction about the singing swan was widely held to be true throughout medieval Europe. Chaucer refers to it, for example. Strange as it may seem, it was also widely believed that in the far north of Europe, men played lyres to attract the swans, who came to join in the performance in great numbers by singing along to the music.

A DEAD-SURE THING—THE SWAN SONG OF DEMOCRACY.

Republican president Teddy Roosevelt swept aside opposition in 1904, hence the rival Democratic Party is shown as a fatally injured swan giving its swan song in this US political cartoon.

The sixteenth-century Italian naturalist Aldrovandus sought proof of the swan's singing ability, and took testimony from an apparently honest Englishman called George Braun, who assured him that nothing was more common in England than to hear swans sing; that they bred in great numbers in the sea near London; and that every fleet of ships that returned from voyages to distant countries was met by swans that came joyfully out to welcome their return, and salute them with a loud and cheerful singing! The unfortunate Aldrovandus clearly believed him, because he published every word.

Shakespeare refers to the song of the dying swan on several occasions. In *Othello*, for example, Emilia says: 'I will play the swan. And die in music.' The poet Samuel Taylor Coleridge had obviously endured a number of dreadful human singers in his time, and could not resist penning the following mischievous lines:

> *Swans sing before they die – 't were no bad thing*
> *Should certain persons die before they sing.*

Coupled with the unusual story that the swan sang as it died, was the belief that swans lived an extraordinarily long time. Seventeenth-century ornithologist Francis Willughby believed that they could live for up to 300 years. Maybe at least partly because of the inaccurate connection with singing, the swan has inspired a great deal of European music. For example, the Finnish composer Sibelius wrote the poignant *Swan of Tuonela* in 1893. Tuonela is the land of the dead in Finnish mythology, and is surrounded by a large black river. Sibelius's expressive music describes a majestic white swan gliding across these dark waters, singing its sorrowful song. Mythology about the swan has stimulated other composers too. Wagner's opera *Lohengrin*, for instance, was completed in 1850 and is a version of the medieval Legend of the Swan Knight who appears in a boat drawn by swans to save a damsel in distress.

Medieval swan in a thirteenth-century English bestiary – contrary to the image here, swans do not eat fish. (*Courtesy of the British Library illuminated manuscripts collection www.bl.uk*)

The most famous classical composition to take inspiration from the swan is, of course, the ballet *Swan Lake*, which premiered in 1877. It is the tragic story of a prince who tries to break a spell that has transformed a beautiful princess and her companions into swans. Tchaikovsky probably took his motivation for this tale from a range of Russian, German and other European folklore. *The Swan* by Saint-Saëns is another celebrated piece with ballet connections. It was written as part of *The Carnival of the Animals* (1886), but later used as music for a solo ballet performance by Anna Pavlova.

The story that some swans are really bewitched young women, or women that can change themselves into swans, is a common tradition. Many such stories are found across Europe and the Middle East, and date back hundreds of years. The women involved are sometimes described by folklorists as 'swan maidens' if they could change their appearance at will, and these beautiful women who could fly may have inspired our popular depiction of angels. There are numerous types of swan maiden tale. A typical example is found in the *Arabian Nights*, where a goldsmith named Hasan secretly watches a group of swans arrive to bathe in a pool. To his surprise, they disrobe and are revealed as beautiful young girls. They change back into their swan costumes and fly away, but Hasan returns to the spot later and waits. This time, after the swans have arrived and undressed, he hides the feather clothing of the girl he has fallen in love with. Unable to fly away, she is locked up by Hassan until she agrees to marry him. They have children and all seems well until one day, several years later, his bride manages to get hold of her feather costume, which Hassan had hidden, and she flies away. But the story has a happy ending because the heartbroken Hassan tracks her down and after many adventures, catches up with her, apologises, and husband and wife are reconciled.

Another well-known example from Ireland concerns the four children of Lir, ruler of the sea. When their mother dies, their new stepmother is jealous of the relationship they have with their father and gets rid of them by changing them into swans for 900 years. The evil stepmother has her comeuppance, but when the spell eventually expires the children rapidly age to their full 900 years and die. Fortunately, a monk is on hand to baptise them before the end so that they are reunited with their father in heaven.

One of the most famous swan transformations in ancient times involved not a female, but a male character. Zeus, the father of the Greek gods, was wont to alter his form and become an animal in order to lure the objects of his desire into a false sense of security, and he had his eye on Leda, the beautiful wife of King Tyndareus of Sparta. Accordingly, Zeus changed himself into a handsome male swan and confronted Leda alone before, somewhat improbably, seducing her.

Various outcomes from this most bizarre sexual union were described by ancient writers, but all agree that Leda was delivered of eggs that later hatched into babies. In a popular version of the legend, one of these infants grew up to become Helen, who sparked the Trojan War with Greece because of her beauty. This whole story was a fashionable subject for art in the Greco-Roman world as well as in later periods such as the Renaissance, where artists could be fairly explicit with their depictions because Leda's consort was a bird rather than a human male.

Leda with Zeus in the guise of a swan. (*Courtesy of Wellcome Library, London*)

There are many other instances of men being transformed into swans in Greek mythology. One version of the death of the legendary musician Orpheus was that his soul was transported into a swan after he was murdered. Similarly, a warrior son of Neptune is turned into a swan by his father when he is killed by Achilles during the Trojan War; a king of Liguria and a son of Apollo are also transformed into swans. The frequency with which the swan appears in Greek mythology may explain why this bird has given its name to a constellation. *Cygnus*, the swan, is one of only three 'classical' constellations identified by Greek astronomer Ptolemy that is named after birds: the others are *Corvus*, the raven, and *Aquila*, the eagle. Since the constellation *Cygnus* is located next to *Lyra*, the lyre, and Orpheus was a renowned player of this instrument, it is tempting to believe that he may have been the main inspiration for the constellation's name.

A well-known children's story about the swan from more recent times is *The Ugly Duckling* by Hans Christian Andersen, published in 1843. When a clutch of eggs under a duck hatch, one of the baby birds is different to the others. He is big, grey and unattractive, and as a result he is mocked and made to feel an outcast. After many tribulations, and much to his surprise, he matures into a beautiful swan. It is a clever allegorical tale about personal identity and not judging by appearances. Given that Andersen was Danish, the mute swan has, rather fittingly, been adopted as the national bird of Denmark.

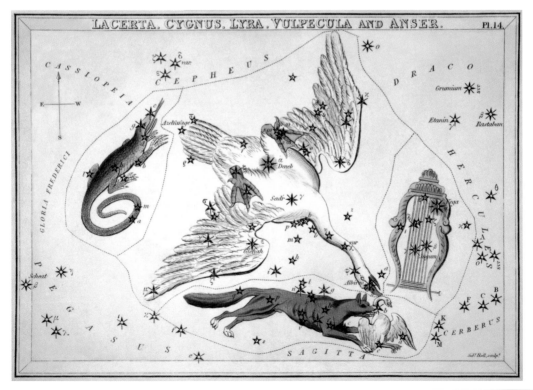

The constellation of the swan (cygnus) next to Orpheus's lyre (lyra).

The noble head of a royal bird on the Thames.

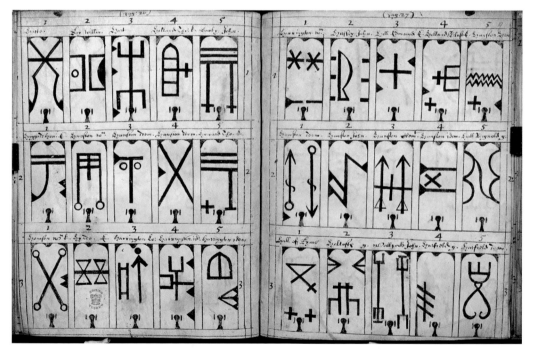

Sixteenth-century swan marks applied to the bird's beaks to illustrate who owned them. (*Courtesy of the British Library illuminated manuscripts collection www.bl.uk*)

Probably the second most oft-quoted assertion about swans, after their alleged ability to break your leg, is that the Royal Family owns them all. How did this come about?

Swans were prized as a delicacy at medieval royal banquets and so, keen to ensure a continued supply, the monarchy asserted its ownership of them as far back as the twelfth century. Another early connection with the bird came after Henry IV married Mary de Bohun. Her family used the swan as an heraldic badge, so Henry and his heirs adopted it. Swans acquired such prestige that Edward IV ruled that only his son or a wealthy man earning more than five marks a year could keep them. Under Henry VII, the punishment for taking their eggs was imprisonment for a year and a day, plus a fine.

In Elizabethan times, the law stated that 'All stray swans, all swans unmarked, all wild swans, all tame swans that fly, all swans of felons … are the Master of the Swans' right.' The Master of the Swans was an office in the royal household, and by Elizabeth's reign there were around 900 legitimate owners of swans sanctioned by the Crown, all with their own swan-marks indicating ownership. Birds were marked with patterns of notches or branding on the bill, or nicks on the webbing of the feet. The monarch still has the right to claim ownership of any unmarked mute swan in open waters.

The Worshipful Company of Dyers and The Worshipful Company of Vintners own swans on the river Thames, together with the monarch. A royal 'swan upping' ceremony is held on the Thames every year to count the swans, and to assess the health and weight of cygnets.

Like the Red Lion and the Royal Oak, the many connections with royalty have helped The Swan to become one of the most popular names for a pub in England.

Woodpecker

Great spotted woodpecker.

*W*oodpeckers are colourful birds with unique wood-chiselling behaviour, and this seems to have suggested to our ancient ancestors that they were in some way special. Maybe they were even linked with the gods themselves. The Romans called the woodpecker by the name *picus*, and held it in particular reverence. The historian Plutarch gives three explanations for this elite status:

Why do the Latins revere the woodpecker and all strictly abstain from [eating] it?

Is it because, as they tell the tale, Picus the son of Saturn, transformed by his wife's magic potions, became a woodpecker and in that form gave oracles and prophecies to those who consulted him?

Or is this wholly incredible and monstrous, and is another tale more credible that relates that when Romulus and Remus [the founders of Rome] were abandoned, not only did a she-wolf suckle them, but also a certain woodpecker came continually to visit them and bring them scraps of food? For generally, even to this day, in foothills and thickly wooded places where the woodpecker is found, there also is found the wolf, as Nigidius records.

Great spotted woodpecker in a Tudor text.

Or is it rather because they regard this bird as sacred to Mars, even as other birds to other gods? For it is a courageous and spirited bird and has a beak so strong that it can overturn oaks by pecking them until it has reached the inmost part of the tree.

The natural historian Pliny confirms Plutarch's assertion that the woodpecker was especially associated with the Roman god of war and thunder, Mars. The drumming sound of the woodpecker's hammering on a tree is perhaps reminiscent of thunder and a number of other ancient religions connect the bird to 'thunder gods'. The Greeks, for example, associated the woodpecker with the king of the gods, Zeus, who is often portrayed clutching a lightning bolt, and the mighty Norse god of thunder, Thor, was also represented by this bird. Pliny stresses that the woodpecker was considered especially important in Roman augury – the art of predicting the future by observing the behaviour of animals. He gives a startling example:

These birds have held the first rank in auguries, in Latium, since the time of the king [Picus] who gave them their name. One of the portents that was given by them, I cannot pass over in silence. A woodpecker came and lighted upon the head of Aelius Tubero, the city praetor [magistrate], when sitting on his tribunal dispensing justice in the Forum, and showed such tameness as to allow itself to be taken with the hand; upon which the augurs declared that if it was let go, the state would be menaced with danger, but if killed, disaster would befall the praetor. In an instant he tore the bird to pieces, and before long the omen was fulfilled.

Roman commentators note that the unfortunate Tubero did pay a high price for destroying the woodpecker and saving the city of Rome – shortly afterwards, seventeen members of his family were killed by Hannibal's army at the Battle of Cannae.

If a woodpecker made its home in a tree it was thought to bestow magical protection upon it. One medieval bestiary asserts that 'if a woodpecker nests in a tree, a nail or anything inserted into the trunk will not rest there for long, but will fall out as soon as the bird sits on its nest.' Some believed that the woodpecker had access to a magical herb that it used for this and other purposes.

There is a wide variety of general regional names for woodpeckers that describe their chiselling activity, including tree-jobber, pick-a-tree, and hew-hole. The green woodpecker has many names, including woodspite, nick-a-pepper, awl bird, and speck. Many of them are imitative of the bird's loud laughing call, such as heyhoe, ecle, yaffle, and hickwall, but a personal favourite is 'Laughing Betsy', which originates from the West Midlands. Yet the bird's characteristic call has another important association: it was believed to be an attempt to call forth rain. Around the world, a number of birds have been designated the rainbird or rainfowl – usually because their voice or behaviour is said to herald a downpour. In the UK, these titles have been most consistently applied to the green woodpecker, which has also been known as the storm cock or storm bird. These latter names have been applied to the mistle thrush as well, since it has a habit of continuing to call even during bad weather.

Woodpecker, spare that spire

A peculiar modern phenomenon is that of woodpeckers attacking British churches. In the late twentieth and early twenty-first centuries, they seem to have become particularly attracted to wooden spires. It may be that the wood of older buildings conceal grubs that the birds seek out, but there may be another explanation. The tall, hollow, dry timber of spires may also make an especially fine 'sounding board' for the drumming that male woodpeckers engage in with their bills to attract a mate. The birds don't seem to nest in the holes they create, but may roost there. Perhaps the loss of native forests and the enticing of woodland birds into town gardens has encouraged this behaviour. Either way, the ravages of determined woodpeckers can be very serious – often leading to repair bills of many tens of thousands of pounds, and some churches even face closure because of the damage.

The problem became so acute at one Norwegian church that the minister was given permission to call in a marksman to shoot the birds responsible.

The woodpecker's association with rain is not unique to the UK – other European countries bestow similar attributes – and Christian legend gives an explanation for the link. It tells how God asked all the birds to help dig out the oceans and rivers before he filled them with water, but the woodpeckers refused. So God cursed them by allowing them only to drink rainwater, and now the birds constantly cry for rain because they are always thirsty.

Given their attractive plumage, it's not too surprising that people in the past tried to keep woodpeckers as pets, since attempts were made to tame almost every other sort of bird. However, for once, even the most ardent bird keepers generally admitted defeat. One early nineteenth-century expert wrote of the green woodpecker:

> The beauty of its plumage is all that can be said of it; for it is so fierce, quick, and stubborn, that it can only be kept by means of a chain. I know no instance in which every kind of attention has rendered it more docile and agreeable: it is always untractable. One or two of these chained birds, however, do not look bad as a variety. It is curious to see them crack the nuts.

Many of the regional names for the other major species of woodpecker in the UK, the great spotted woodpecker, utilise the word 'pie' to reflect its primarily black and white colouration. Examples include wood pie and pied woodpecker. One old name, 'French pie', probably reflects the fact that green woodpeckers were once much more numerous and so considered the native species, with the great spotted variety viewed as an invader from the Continent.

Inspired animation

One of the most famous cartoon birds in history is the zany and eccentric Woody Woodpecker. Walter Lantz was the US animator who created Woody, but his artistic inspiration came at a rather unexpected time. While on honeymoon with his wife Grace in a forest cabin, the couple were constantly distracted by an overly attentive woodpecker who perpetually poked nuts under the eaves, pecked at the roof, and uttered its screaming call. It was Grace who suggested that this crazy bird would make a great cartoon character, and this led to Woody's first appearance in 1940. Grace herself later voiced Woody and his famous laugh.

Green woodpecker.

Index